Front Range
Topropes

rienne Regamey toproping on a busy day at Turkey Rocks

Front Range Topropes, Second Edition

ISBN   1-892540-13-4

Front Cover Photo: Melissa Lester on the Rock Island in Boulder Canyon. Photo by Fred Knapp.

Inside Photos: Most uncredited photos are by Heidi or Fred Knapp. Some cliff photos are by Mike Stevens. Several of the Table Mountain photos are by Stewart Green. Some action photos by Dan Hare.

The excellent maps were created by Stece "Crusher" Bartlett.

Thanks to the many people who have helped with this book: Teri Ebel for suggesting the idea; Heidi Knapp for helping with everything from typing to production; my sister Sonia for checking mileages and proof reading; Stewart Green for showing me around the Garden of the Gods and letting me use his excellent photos; Dan Hare for photos and developing most of the routes in Boulder Canyon; Mike Stevens for the original help with Boulder Topropes; Mark Day for the countless suggestions that will certainly lead to the success of Sharp End; Steve "Crusher" Bartlett for all his map expertise and hard work; and the many advertisers who support the climbing community and this book: The Bent Gate, The Boulder Rock Club, The Mountain Shop, Mountain Miser, Mountain Sports, Neptune Mountaineering, Paradise Rock Gym, and Petzl.

Printed in the United States of America.

For more information or to order books contact:
Sharp End Publishing   (303) 444-2698
P.O. Box 1613   www.sharpendbooks.com
Boulder, CO 80306-1613   inforock@aol.com

Read This Before Using This Guide Book

Rock climbing, including toproping, is extremely dangerous. A small and incomplete list of possible dangers includes: loose rock, weather, anchor failure (fixed anchors, natural anchors, and removable protection), dangerous pendulums, equipment failure, etc.

THE AUTHOR AND PUBLISHER EXPRESSLY DISCLAIM ALL REPRESENTATIONS AND WARRANTIES REGARDING THIS GUIDE, THE ACCURACY OF THE INFORMATION CONTAINED HEREIN, AND THE RESULTS OF YOUR USE HEREOF, INCLUDING WITHOUT LIMITATION, IMPLIED WARRANTIES OF MERCHANTABILITY AND FITNESS FOR A PARTICULAR PURPOSE. THE USER ASSUMES ALL RISK ASSOCIATED WITH THE USE OF THIS GUIDE.

It is your responsibility to take care of yourself while climbing. Seek a professional instructor or guide if you are unsure of your ability to handle any circumstances that may arise. This guide is not intended as an instructional manual.

TABLE OF CONTENTS

INTRODUCTION

The most frequently asked question at any Front Range climbing shop is "Where can I go to toprope?" Most Colorado climbing areas aren't blessed with an abundance of concentrated easy-to-toprope cliffs. Over the past year and a half, I have worked to ferret out the premier toprope areas in the region from Fort Collins to Colorado Springs. In addition to finding whole crags conducive to toproping, I've included classic routes in popular areas such as Eldorado Canyon, Rocky Mountain National Park, and Garden of the Gods.

It is my hope and intention to encourage climbers to explore areas away from their home towns, to pack up for a day or a weekend and venture to different rock and different regions. Most of all, I want climbers to have fun and be careful. If an approach to an anchor looks dicey, find another climb. While I've done my darndest to get all the accurate information, my perceptions may be different from yours. If you notice any errors or know of other quality topropes that I've omitted, please contact Sharp End Publishing, P.O. Box 1613, Boulder, CO 80306-1613.

Enjoy the great climbing of Colorado's Front Range.

To Heidi,
my soulmate,
for her nearly
unfathomable
love and
support.

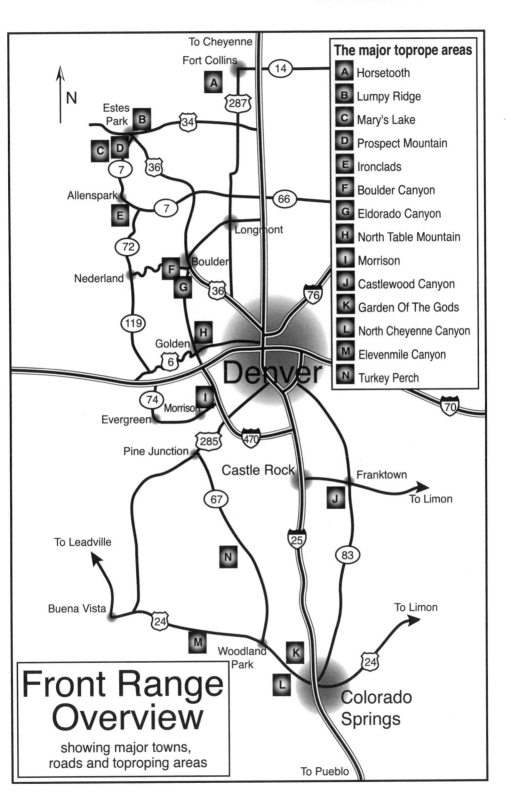

How To Use This Guide

Front Range Topropes follows the natural lines of The Front Range moving north to south. This book is divided up by city, climbing area, then by crag.

For example, the Boulder Area is described as a city; Boulder Canyon is a climbing area; Happy Hour is a crag.

Icons are used to express pertinent information in the simplest manner. On cliffs where a variety of anchors are needed, climbs are often given their own symbols. On more concentrated cliffs, such as those of Castlewood Canyon or North Table Mountain, the icons often apply to whole crags because so many routes have the same requirements.

Route names and ratings are listed under the appropriate crags. Ratings are expressed using the Yosemite Decimal System.

In several instances, gear is required to set up a feasible toprope. While this may prove out of the reach of beginning climbers, a few nuts and camming units, and knowledge of how to place them, can provide the only anchor. Most routes in this guide, however, are arranged from natural anchors (trees or boulders) or bolts.

Topos, Photos, & Icons

This guide is not intended as an instructional manual. While toproping may be safer than other manifestations of rock climbing, it is still a dangerous endeavor requiring knowhow and experience. The information in this guide will help steer experienced climbers to toproping opportunities in what is arguably the world's most magnificent climbing area.

This guidebook relies on the use of icons to indicate the difficulty of the approach, the angle of the route, difficulty reaching the toprope anchor, gear requirements, and child safety at the base.

Approach Information

Easy Approach: Less than 10 minutes and/or easy hiking.

Moderate Approach: 15-30 minutes and/or some steep terrain.

Difficult Approach: An hour or more of hiking and/or steep terrain.

Anchor Information

Natural Anchors: Nearby trees and/or boulders make suitable anchors. Back up with gear when possible.

Gear Anchors: Bring your own pro to set up anchors.

Bolt Anchors: Bolts are in place. Know how to judge their safety and back them up when possible.

Child Safety Information

Kids Safe: Nature of the crag lends itself to being relatively safe for kids.

Kids Unsafe: Loose rock or unstable talus create dangers for children. Proximity to road may also be a factor.

Anchor Access Information

Easy Access: Top of the crag and/ or anchors are easily accessible with nothing more than a short hike.

Moderate Access: Some scrambling may be necessary to reach the top and/or the anchors.

Difficult Access: At least 3rd class and sometimes 4th class scrambling required to reach the top. Belays recommended. Rappels may be involved.

Rock Angle Information

Slabby Climbing: Routes tend to be on rock less than 90 degrees.

Vertical Climbing: Routes tend to be vertical in nature.

Steep Climbing: Routes tend to be overhanging.

Child Safety Note:
Parents should check out the cliff in advance and evaluate the safety of the surroundings, as the nature of crags is generally unsafe.

Sonia Knapp jamming S Crack

FORT COLLINS AREA/ HORSETOOTH RESERVOIR

Horsetooth Reservoir, the famed bouldering area of Fort Collins, is also home to the city's best toproping. The Dakota sandstone provides interesting featured rock complete with classic crack lines and phenomenal face routes. With a backdrop of the reservoir and ample summer swimming opportunity, Horsetooth is a climbing site well worth visiting. The longest topropes are found near the western terminus of Duncan's Ridge, but the shorter walls of the Torture Chamber and Rotary Park also offer great climbs.

Horsetooth can be approached from the south by taking Horsetooth Road or by following Road 42C from Overland Drive. For the Torture Chamber park at a pull-out on Horsetooth Rd. just before the intersection with Road 23 (the road that runs along the reservoir). For Duncan's Ridge park on the eastern parking area on the north side of Spring Canyon Dam. Rotary Park is accessed from a paved parking area on the west side of the road 1.3 miles north of the intersection of 23 & 42C.

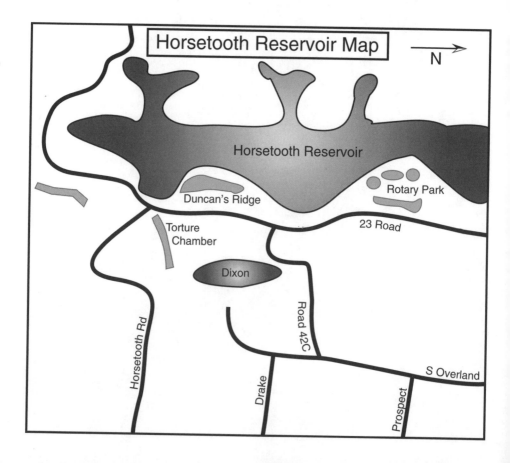

DUNCAN'S RIDGE

Duncan's Ridge is the long rib of rock that runs along the inlet formed by the Spring Canyon Dam. This area contains the most concentrated number of topropes. The entire cliff band lends itself to toproping and a busy weekend will see parties experimenting with various uncharted routes along the eastern part of the ridge. Bringing a light rack, some long slings, and a sense of adventure will ensure a fun day on this unchartered section. For those seeking direction, this guide describes the most popular established routes at the western terminus.

To get to the described toprope area, follow a trail near the ridge top for about a half mile. Near the end of the cliffs, several hundred yards south of a private residence, is the tallest section of cliff. A large tree serves as an anchor for two routes, while gear is required for the others. An easy scramble can be found between the two biggest trees, at the northern end of the crag.

The rock in this area is composed of a medium grained conglomerate that provides excellent friction on the face routes and some painful jams on the cracks. While the area is safe for children, the short scramble might be limiting for younger kids.

DUNCAN'S RIDGE TOPROPES

1. **Easy Slabs** 5.2-5.4
2. **Overhang Route** 5.8
3. **Broken Crack** 5.6
4. **Conglomerate Face** 5.8
5. **Dihedral Route** 5.7
6. **Roof Route** 5.10
7. **Corner Climb** 5.9
8. **5.10 Face**
9. **Crack Climb** 5.9

Kevin Schaefer on the Dihedral Route.

Duncan's Ridge

THE ROTARY PARK BOLT WALL

The Bolt Wall is located only a short walk from the Rotary Park parking area and is home to some phenomenal toprope problems. From the main parking area, walk down to the cliffs and continue south along the top. Two pairs of ring-bolt anchors serve as protection for *Corner Cling* and *Cat's Eye*. The numerous boulders can be tied off to toprope other routes.

1. Easy Does It 5.5
The clean albeit short slabs on the left side of the wall.
2. Classic Crack 5.9
The pin-scarred dihedral.
3. The Faces 5.9
The clean wall can be toproped at 5.9 or made harder via eliminates.
4. Classic Dihedral 5.10
The beautiful dihedral right of the bolt holes is an excellent climb with the crux down low.
5. West Bulge 5.10
Another low crux is found on the face right of *Classic Dihedral*.
6. Cat's Eye 5.10d
Climb the smooth face and gain an undercling crack that leads to the top.
7. Corner Cling 5.9
Begin left of the clean Indian Creek-esque crack on the right side of a flake. Continue left out of an undercling.
8. Classic Flake 5.7
This is the right side of the flake. You'll risk a long swing if you're using the bolt anchors. The rating only applies to the climbing up to the roof.

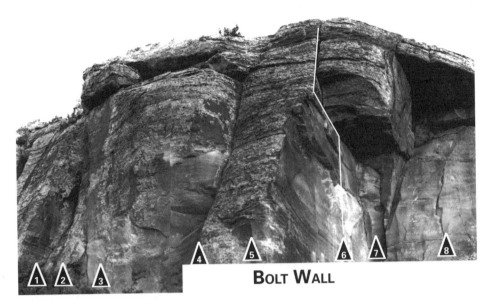

Bolt Wall

Nemesis Tower & Torture Chamber

The Torture Chamber isn't nearly as bad as the name implies. Though not as tall as the larger faces of Duncan's Ridge, the area is home to many of Horsetooth's better crack lines. The best approach to the Chamber is found by parking about a block east of the intersection of 23 Road and Horsetooth, near a roadcut. Access to the base of the cliffs can be found early on as you hike along the rim to the Nemesis Tower, identified from above as a large block separated from the cliff. The routes lie on and between Nemesis Tower and the ridge's eastern terminus. Though the approach is rather short, it requires a short scramble and wouldn't be great for small children.

Nemesis Tower

1. West Crack 5.8
An obvious crack on the formation's west side.

2. West Flake 5.9
A flake immediately left of *West Crack*.

Crack Wall

5.9

5.8

Nemesis Tower

3. Nemesis Standard B2 (something like 12d)
The scoop-like face left of *West Flake*.
4. North Arete
5. Northeast Face 5.11a
Start up a small corner and move right to the *North Arete*.
6. Dihedral Line 5.11a
Climb the classic finger corner left of #5.

CRACK WALL
7. The Thin One 5.11
Downhill from Nemesis and left of a prominent tree.
8. S Crack 5.10d
As the name implies....
9. Crack in Groove 5.8
10. Cracky Face 5.10d
Just left of *S Crack*.
11. Final Finger 5.10c

Numerous other crack and face climbs are not shown on the topo, as they aren't known by name.

Strappo Hughes setting up a toprope the hard way on the Baby Twin Owls
Steve "Crusher" Bartlett photo

ESTES PARK AREA

Estes Park, the gateway to Rocky Mountain National Park, is a global destination for outdoor enthusiasts, nature lovers, and rock climbers. Anyone living on the Front Range can appreciate its cool high altitude weather in the midst of a scorching summer. The high country, despite its afternoon thunderstorms, provides a great escape from the warmer metro areas.

While Rocky Mountain Park, with its lofty summits, is the most famous of the climbing destinations near Estes, an amazing number of small crags abound. Mary's Lake is stacked with convenient short topropes and curbside belays. Prospect Mountain provides a bit more solitude and a few longer endeavors. The Punk Rock, near Allenspark, offers excellent and convenient toproping in a mountain setting. And of course, the smaller rocks of Lumpy Ridge allow for topropes in the National Park.

The town of Estes, packed in the summer, provides all the amenities a visitor could want. Great day hikes can round out a day at the crags while the restaurants can round out your waistline. Quick eats include the Fruit Shake (smoothies) and the Notchtop Cafe (coffee and sandwiches). Sit down meals abound.

If you haven't yet climbed in the Estes area, or if you haven't checked out the many hidden gems described in this guide, it's time you did.

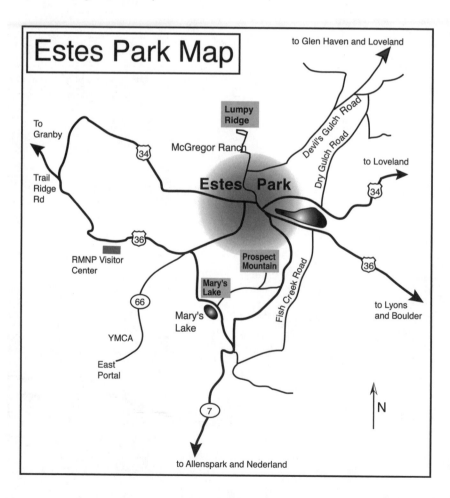

LUMPY RIDGE

Lumpy Ridge is the premier climbing area in Rocky Mountain National Park. Known for its long flaring cracks, the area isn't graced with an abundance of topropes. The exceptions to this rule are tropropes conveniently located near the parking area.

LITTLE TWIN OWLS

This feature, easily viewed from the parking lot, is home to two great, albeit difficult, toprope problems. Get to the summit via a wide, easy fifth-class crack.

1. Finger Crack 5.11
2. Face Route 5.11

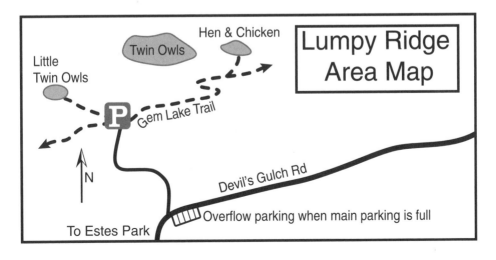

THE HEN & THE CHICKEN

Though the approach may be rather long, the Hen and the Chicken, satellite features of the Twin Owls, possess some topropable routes. This buttress is located at the eastern edge of the East Owl and is best approached by following the Gem Lake Trail until it becomes obvious to cut upwards. *Yosemite Crack*, a fabulous 5.10c on the East Owl, is the main toprope attraction to this area. A word of caution: setting up these topropes is a bit hairy and directionals are helpful on several of the routes on the main wall. Think of this as an advanced toprope crag.

Hen & Chicken

East Owl

Yosemite Crack 5.10c
(hidden in this
photo)

Left Side
Topropes

1. Rooster Tail 5.9+

It is best to follow the left-hand variant when the crack forks towards the top. Weird to toprope given the swing, but possible.

2. Hagakure 5.12a

A sustained seam with occasional fixed gear. Another weird TR problem.

3. Cackle Crack 5.8

A left-facing dihedral that's worth the walk.

4. Rhode Island Red 5.10a

The crack a few feet right of *Cackle Crack.*

5. Left Side Topropes 5.6-5.8

Several cracks on the left side of the Hen & Chicken can be toproped. Difficulty is based on eliminates.

6. Yosemite Crack 5.10c

This is the hand and fist crack about 60 feet left of the Hen & the Chicken. True hard man training for the Big Ditch in California.

Left Side Topropes

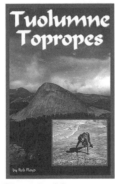

PROSPECT MOUNTAIN

The Thumb and the Thimble are two of the prominent rocks that rise from the eastern flanks of Prospect Mountain, due south of downtown Estes Park. To reach this area take Highway 7 to Peak View Drive. Continue 1.0 miles to a dirt road (making sure not to fork right on Devon Road). Follow the dirt road for 0.7 miles to a pullout for two cars before a gate. (If this parking space is full, park on Peak View Drive and walk up the road). Look for a foot trail rather than hiking up the giant gully. A five minute walk leads to the cliffs.

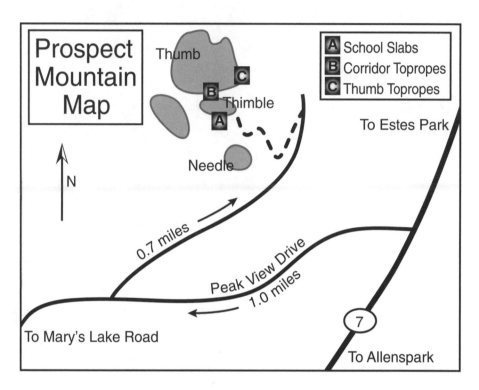

THE THUMB & THE THIMBLE

The Thumb and the Thimble are popular training areas for local guides. The School Slabs in particular are easily accessed and offer climbs from 5.3 to 5.7, with the harder routes being toward the right side. The back side of the School Slabs is a narrow corridor that houses more difficult routes on a vertical but short wall. To the right of this corridor are several routes of greater length and continuity, but access to their bolt anchors is guarded by some 5.4 climbing.

The Thimble

The Thumb

The Thumb Topropes 5.4 - 5.8

Bolt anchors on ledge

A. School Slabs 5.3-5.7
These routes are accessed via a scramble on the east side. Routes get harder from left to right.

B. Corridor Topropes 5.7
Steep and short climbs on the Thimble with many variations. Same access as School Slabs.

C. Thumb Topropes 5.4-5.8
These are great climbs but to get to the anchor bolts one must climb the 5.4 beginning off a pedestal.

Carrie Mayers on School Slabs

MARY'S LAKE

Mary's Lake is reached by driving South from Estes Park on Highway 34 (South St. Vrain Ave.) for 3.4 miles to a turnoff for Mary's Lake. Follow this road for another 0.7 miles to a pullout on the right. This same spot can also be reached by taking Mary's Lake Road and driving 2.0 miles from Moraine.

The rocks of Mary's Lake are essentially a group of large boulders. The area is used by the YMCA as a teaching location and many of the climbs have bolt anchors on top. Many of the bolts, however, lack hangers, so it is necessary to bring keyhole hangers or wired stoppers to utilize these anchors.

THE CORRIDOR

The Corridor is the furthest south and west of the toproping areas at Mary's Lake. Topropes vary in length from 20 feet (on the south wall) to 40 feet (on the north wall).

1. South Wall 5.10
Climb the steep wall via several variations. Steep and sustained despite the length.

2. Black Dog Runs at Night 5.10c
This is the steep prow that faces NW. It was bolted as a lead, but only one bolt remains as a directional.

3. North Wall 5.6-5.8
A less than vertical wall of greater length than the *South Wall*. Many variations exist. The various difficulties should be obvious.

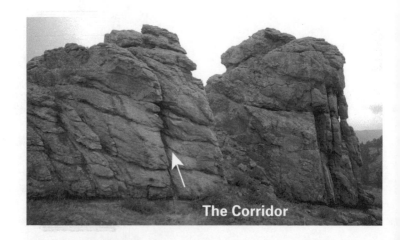

The Corridor

West Face of Eastern Block

The top of the cliff is gained by a 3rd class scramble up a cleft on the east face.

Eastern Block

1. Unknown 5.8
A good delicate route.

2. Crack Route 5.8
A good route that follows a tricky crack.

3. Roof Route 5.8
A good route that follows a tricky crack.

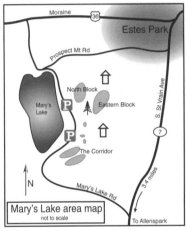

Mary's Lake area map
not to scale

North Rock

The North Rock has some interesting short topropes in the 5.6-5.8 range. As a general rule, the routes get harder as one moves right.

North Rock

THE IRONCLADS

This great-for-toproping area near Allenspark is well worth a visit, especially during the warm summer months. Though several sport climbing crags exist in this area, the Punk Rock (aka Poacher's Rock) and Mount Boner are the most convenient for toproping. Punk Rock is, in fact, set up with two sets of anchors — a high one that offers safe rigging as well as lower sport-convenience anchors.

The routes shown on the Punk Rock photo are the bolted routes on the west face; however, it is certainly possible to toprope the shorter east face from the upper anchors. Slabs to the south appear to hold promise for great climbing. Bring long slings and protection if you're up for experimenting with virgin rock.

To reach the Ironclads, head south from Allenspark on Highway 7 to mile marker 18.8, located just before the Hilltop Guild. Follow the main road for one mile, and just as the trees on the left open up into a large aspen grove, take a right and proceed until Punk Rock is visible. You can practically park beneath the routes. In fact, the reason the bottom right part of the top photo is covered is to hide my car.

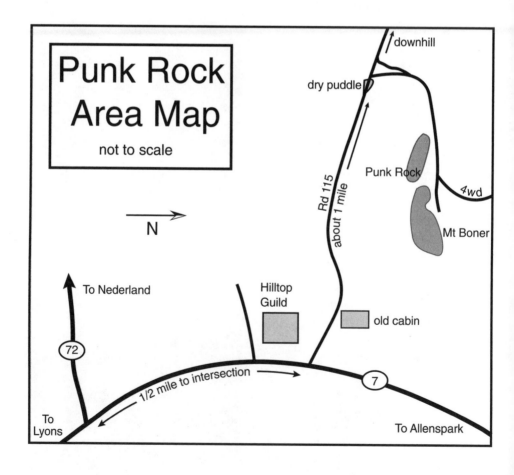

Punk Rock/Poacher's Rock

This sport crag is also conveniently set up for toproping. The routes are on excellent granite in a secluded high country setting.

Punk Rock
(more bolts on top)

1. Seething Bitch 5.8
A good outing. Anchors are to the right of the easier finish.
2. Tuition Dollars at Work 5.11c
A difficult undertaking that doesn't have convenient anchors.
3. Short Take 5.10b/c
Cold-shut anchors identify this route.
4. Blah Blah Blah 5.11a
This route climbs past the brown hangers. Use anchors on #5.
5. Five Finger Discount 5.9
Three bolts and a cold-shut anchor.
6. Short Stop 5.10
Climbs past a small roof.
7. Short Sighted 5.8
Anchors only.
8. Rip Off Ranger 5.9
9. Stock-Still and Stoic 5.10b

Heidi Knapp on Seething Bitch

Melissa Lester starting up a difficult variation on the Rock Island on the Boulder Creek path

BOULDER

Boulder, Colorado has long been the climbing capital of Colorado, if not the nation. The region is blessed with an abundance of rock and rock types. Climbers interested in granite should venture to Boulder Canyon. The Fountain Formation sandstone of the Flatirons and Eldorado Canyon will tempt those who enjoy steep edging.

After more than ten years working at Boulder's most esteemed climbing shops, I've heard the question over and over: "Where can I go to toprope?" Though Boulder's toprope areas are spread throughout a large area, many excellent crags exist. Take time to explore some of the less popular cliffs. The quality will be the same as the roadside crags, and you'll avoid the crowded weekend fray.

If you're visiting Boulder, take advantage of the local culture. The Boulder Mountaineer, Neptune Mountaineering, and Mountain Sports host weekly slide shows, often free. The Pearl Street mall bustles with entertainment and good food, and the area's many trails are worth exploring.

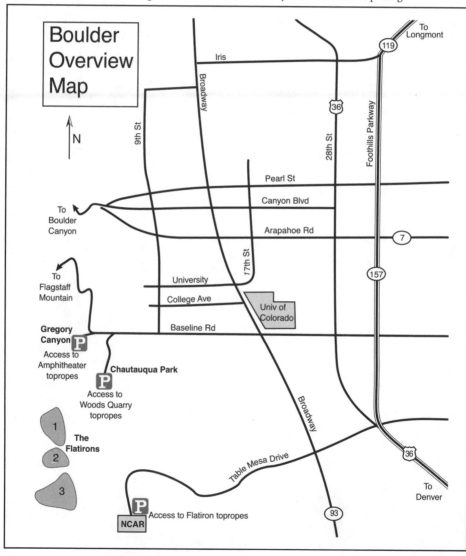

BOULDER CANYON

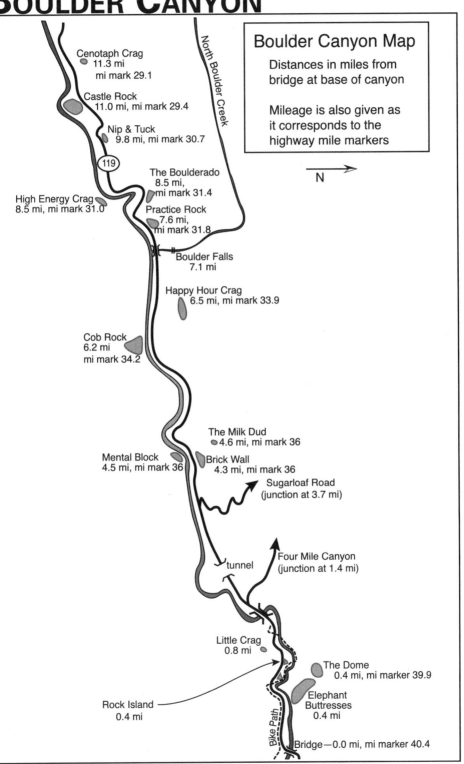

Boulder Canyon Map

Distances in miles from
bridge at base of canyon

Mileage is also given as
it corresponds to the
highway mile markers

N →

North Boulder Creek

Cenotaph Crag
11.3 mi
mi mark 29.1

Castle Rock
11.0 mi, mi mark 29.4

Nip & Tuck
9.8 mi, mi mark 30.7

119

The Boulderado
8.5 mi,
mi mark 31.4

High Energy Crag
8.5 mi, mi mark 31.0

Practice Rock
7.6 mi,
mi mark 31.8

Boulder Falls
7.1 mi

Happy Hour Crag
6.5 mi, mi mark 33.9

Cob Rock
6.2 mi
mi mark 34.2

The Milk Dud
4.6 mi, mi mark 36

Mental Block
4.5 mi, mi mark 36

Brick Wall
4.3 mi, mi mark 36

Sugarloaf Road
(junction at 3.7 mi)

Four Mile Canyon
(junction at 1.4 mi)

tunnel

Little Crag
0.8 mi

The Dome
0.4 mi, mi marker 39.9

Elephant
Buttresses
0.4 mi

Rock Island
0.4 mi

Bike Path

Bridge—0.0 mi, mi marker 40.4

BOULDER CANYON

Boulder Canyon offers some excellent toprope climbing on quality granite. With access provided via a two lane highway, approaches are limited, for the most part, to a 10-15 minute walk. Some of the crags even lie just 20 feet off the highway!

To get to Boulder Canyon, take Canyon Blvd. west out of Boulder (see Boulder map). Reset your trip meter as you cross the bridge over the creek. All mileages to the crags are referenced from this point. Additionally, you may use the mile markers in the canyon as refernces.

The main obstacle to be aware of is North Boulder Creek. Many of the crags are located on the "other" side of the creek, and one may have to ford this to reach a particular destination. In the case of some of the crags, a bridge or stepping stone path leads the way. For others, just roll up those pants and wade across. PLEASE BEWARE: NORTH BOULDER CREEK CAN RUN VERY HIGH AND FAST, PARTICULARLY IN LATE SPRING AND EARLY SUMMER (MAY-JULY). CROSSING WITHOUT BENEFIT OF A BRIDGE DURING THESE TIMES IS STRONGLY DISCOURAGED.

THE ELEPHANT BUTTRESSES & ROCK ISLAND

The Elephant Buttresses are the first crags encountered in Boulder Canyon. These are the prominent tall rocks that face mostly west. The Rock Island is the roadcut crag directly on the bike path near the bridge. The popular topropes on the rock face north. There are pullouts on both sides of the road at mile marker 39.9, less than a mile up the canyon. To reach the Elephant Buttresses, park here, walk north, and cross the bridge. Take a foot trail to the right until a climbing access sign points to a steep trail. Follow this for about 100 yards to its intersection with a small stream. A path on the stream's uphill side takes one to a water pipe. Head south along the water pipe (be very careful walking along this, as a slip could produce quite a fall in some areas!) until the base of the buttresses is reached. Beware of poison ivy in the summer months. Scramble up the obvious gullies just north of the buttresses to gain the summits and set up anchors.

The Elephant Buttresses are numbered one through four, with the northernmost buttress being number one, the southernmost number four. The large granite dome is The Dome — a great crag but with no toproping to speak of.

ROCK ISLAND

1. Independent Route 5.7
Climb up a dihedral or the arete at the start and continue to an anchor of slings around a boulder or gear.

2. Eskimo Roll 5.9

This is the leftmost start of the three routes that share the bolt anchors. The upper crux is a bit stiffer than the rest of the route. Taking the right line at the top is easiest.

3. Rock Island Line 5.9

Start in the center of the bottom wall and join *Eskimo Roll*.

4. Adventures on Rollerblades 5.10

If you're on a roll, try this route. Start at the right side of the wall and climb difficult terrain. For consistency, try one of the more difficult upper finishes rather than skirting up the right side of the overhanging upper headwall.

First Buttress

FIRST BUTTRESS

1. Flash Dihedral 5.8+

Begin on a broken pile 50 feet above the water pipe, and follow the shallow dihedral on the NW face (30-40 ft. slings).

SECOND BUTTRESS - LEFT SIDE

On the Second Buttress it is a very difficult scramble from the belay cove to the summit. When finished climbing, either scramble down to the pipe (ultra desperate) and walk around to the summit to clean your anchors, or better, get belayed up from the top.

2. Tough Situation 5.9

Approach by scrambling up the easy broken gully to a good belay stance just below the angular summit block (10-20 ft. slings).

3. Classic Finger Crack 5.9

Same belay stance as above. Take the obvious stellar finger crack up the face of the summit block.

SECOND BUTTRESS - MAIN FACE

4. Pine Tree Route 5.4-5.5

Ascend the varied face directly below the tree. 60m rope recommended (5 -10 ft. slings).

belay cove

Second Buttress

THIRD BUTTRESS

The routes on the Third Buttress begin up the gully which divides the Second Buttress from the Third.

5. Wingtip 5.10 c/d

Begin 75 feet up the gully under a shallow roof. Turn it (5.9), then take the overhanging left-facing corner. Gain a nice ledge, then finish over easier ground. (20-30 ft. slings).

6. Left Wing 5.10 b/c

Begin 75 feet up the gully on a ledge. Take the leaning left- facing dihedral, then break left past two bolts. Keep heading left where the route roofs out, then turn the final roof near the top. Gain the ledge mentioned above, and finish on easy ground. Please note: there is big swing potential on this route! (20-30 ft. slings).

FOURTH BUTTRESS

The Fourth Buttress sports a fine NW wall which is easily toproped from the summit. A 60m rope is nice. Do not approach via the pipe! Instead, follow the creek, then hike up to the base.

7. Zolar Czakl 5.10a

Begin up a flake in the back of the cave, head right a bit, then straight up over 5.9 terrain to the top. (30-40 ft. slings).

8. Northwest Face 5.8+

Begin level with where the pipe heads into the cave, and traverse right over 3rd class terrain. Follow a line up and slightly left, picking up a broken left-facing corner halfway up. (30-40 ft. slings).

9. The Heartland 5.9+

Begin as for route #8, but keep traversing right. Climb into a difficult thin crack which terminates at a broken ledge. Pick up another thin crack left of the very large dihedral and follow it to the top. Set up anchors as far out on the access ledge as possible. (20-30 ft. slings).

Note: There is a nice smaller cliff above and behind the 4th buttress with some topropes in the moderate range. This is a great spot to do some exploring.

LITTLE CRAG

Little Crag is one of Boulder Canyon's hidden gems. The routes, though short, are on excellent rock. The cliff is rarely crowded and offers great views upcanyon. Though difficult to see from the road, it benefits from being the only climbable piece of rock in the vicinity. Park at the large pullout just past mile 0.8 and walk along the guardrail to the second "yellow arrow." Follow a faint trail up a gully to the cliff. For the most part, the bolt anchors are adequate. Long slings or gear will help with toproping Belladonnna.

1. Belladonna 5.10

The left-angling crack on the NW face.

2. Short But Cute 5.10

From the shallow right-facing corner just right of the prow head up the face.

3. Nothing to Fear 5.10c

Begin up the same shallow corner as for the previous route, but head right halfway up it and pass a horn. Finish up the featured face.

4. Cool Operator 5.11d

Begin on the SW face and climb a right-facing corner. At its top, head right along cracks and features to the top.

THE BRICK WALL

The Brick Wall is a wonderful toproping crag, and for those who don't enjoy long approaches, this is for you, as The Brick Wall is just off the highway.

1. The Perfect Route 5.10

The bottom left part of the face forms a bowl. Climb straight up the middle of this, then bear left below a small A-shaped roof. Continue up the left side of the face.

2. Living On The Edge 5.11b/c

Begin as for #1, but tackle the small roof straight on. From here, continue up the difficult prow to the bulge and the top.

3. The South Face 5.10b

Begin on the right side of the lower slab and climb straight up to a horizontal fracture. Head left here, then cruise straight up and out the bulge.

MENTAL BLOCK

Mental Block is just a bit further up the canyon than The Brick Wall. Wade across the creek at low water. Scramble up the right side to set up anchors.

1. Love Or Confusion 5.11a/b

Begin on the left side of the face and climb into a short right-facing corner. Turn the roof where it ends and head up and right to finish.

2. Obsessive-compulsive 5.12

Downhill and right of #1, an incipient crack almost reaches the ground. Climb up into this, then pick a finish after it peters out at the roof.

3. Manic-depressive 5.11d

The fun route names continue...right of #2, locate a discontinuous crack that again nearly reaches the ground. Follow it up past a couple of pins, turn the roof/bulge, and continue straight up past a bolt.

4. Sleeper 5.12a/b

A stout test. Fifteen feet right of #3, gain a crack which leads up into a small roof. Bypass the roof on its right edge, pick up another crack, and head through another roof to the anchors.

COB ROCK

Cob Rock is one of Boulder Canyon's most popular destinations for multi-pitch climbs. It is not famous for its toproping, but there are three routes worth doing. All of the toproping takes place on a small block at the bottom of the north face. A tyrolean traverse facilitates a creek crossing during high water. Approach from the left side, and cross a somewhat scary (but short) 4th class slab to reach the anchor spots.

***While the base may be good for kids, the river crossing poses a danger.*

1. Night Vision 5.10b

Climb the far left edge of the block. Clip the bolts for directionals (to avoid a long swing) when toproping this.

2. Huston Crack 5.8+
A very famous line. Take the left-most crack. Good wide crack (including some off-width) technique primer.

3. Aid Crack 5.10d
The next crack over from *Huston Crack* (10-20 ft. slings).

4. Face Route 5.11a
Climb the face anywhere to the right of *Aid Crack* (10-20 ft. slings).

HAPPY HOUR CRAG

Happy Hour is one of Boulder's most visited toprope destinations, and for good reason: the crag is perfectly proportioned for toproping, and access to the top is very easy. Nonetheless, a recent climbing fatality serves as a reminder of how dangerous toproping can be.

Park on the south side of the road and slog up the short but steep hill. Happy Hour is easily seen from the road. Small children may have a rough time on the loose scree. Also, beware of poison ivy on the approach. There are two separate sets of bolts on top of Happy Hour. These are located on top of route 3 and route 12. Other anchors can be made with the plentiful trees and boulders on top. All of the routes on Happy Hour are topropeable. See the photo for locations and features. 10-30 ft. slings work for all routes.

1. I, Robot 5.7
Fun lower-angle face climbing on the left end of the cliff.

2. Are We Not Men 5.7
Begin up the right-facing corner behind the tree.

3. Twofers 5.8
Takes on a large roof with interesting knobs.

4. Twofers Gully 5.6
Avoids the roof on the previous route.

5. The Big Spit 5.9
This takes the line on the left side of the *Rush Hour* roof.

6. Rush Hour 5.11+
An extremely difficult boulder problem crux now that holds have broken.

7. Last Call 5.9
Start as for *Dementia* but move left before the beautiful dihedral.

8. Dementia 5.10a
THE classic dihedral.

9. Malign 5.7
The dihedral right of *Dementia*.

10. Tipsey 5.9
Start up *Malign* but head left up a thin crack. The bolted variation beneath this route is *Cheers* (5.10a).

11. Nightcap 5.8+
A classic technical corner route that will challenge your footwork.

12. Skid Row 5.9+
Begin as for *Grins* but move left. Probably not a great toprope problem.

13. Grins 5.8
Climb up and right over a tooth to a technical stemming corner crux.

13a. Last Laugh 5.10d

Not pictured but clearly defined as the bolted finish to *Grins*.

14. Hands Off 5.7

The big right-facing corner.

15. The Great Race 5.9+

16. Baby Aliens 5.12a

Almost no one leads this anyway.

17. Bad Sneakers 5.9+

Brilliant corner climbing.

18. Cruel Shoes 5.9

The rightmost corner.

PRACTICE ROCK

Practice Rock is another of Boulder's most visited toprope crags. The approach couldn't be easier, as Practice Rock lies right on the road. 10-20 ft. slings.

1. Left Crack 5.9+

The obvious crack up the left side.

2. Almost Left Crack 5.9-

The crack just right of #1.

3. Regular Route 5.11b

The brilliant zig-zag crack up the middle. Pin scar practice for the Valley.

4. Lieback 5.10a

The obvious wide flake on the right side of the face.

THE BOULDERADO

The Boulderado is a very appealing cliff just up the canyon from Practice Rock. Moderate routes dominate this slab, but there are some very challenging steep routes up the far right side. *Q's, Jazz on the Mezzanine,* and *Suite 11* have bolt anchors; the rest of the routes rely on gear or natural anchors. 10-20 ft. slings take care of all the anchors.

1. Jam It 5.8
Follow a nice hand crack through a roof.

2. Ho Hum 5.4
An easy right-facing dihedral.

3. Idle Hands 5.6
Probably the best line. Climb up the middle to a crack, then tackle the steeper headwall.

4. Mons 5.5
Take the crack right of *Idle Hands.*

5. Fistula 5.3
The wide crack right of *Mons.*

6. Q's 5.9+
Just right of the gully that separates the slabby section from the steep section. Follows a bolt line to a three bolt anchor.

7. Jazz on the Mezzanine 5.12b
Start right of the arete, then climb up to it. Three-bolt anchor.

8. Suite 11 5.11b/c
This line tackles the steep, thin crack on the SW wall.

HIGH ENERGY CRAG

High Energy Crag is obvious from the highway. All of the climbing is on the blocky upper crag, which is accessed via the slabs below. The routes begin where the slab meets the blocks. Bring 30 foot slings.

1. No Preservatives 5.10c
Climb the shallow dihedral that lies left of the large block on the lower left side (20-30 ft. slings).

2. Star Span 5.11b/c
Climb the crack that goes up the right side of the block mentioned in #1 (10-20 ft. slings).

3. Golden Bull 5.10b/c

Seventy feet right of *Star Span*, climb the crack just right of the overhanging arete formed by the large block.

4. Proton 5.9

A few feet to the right from *Golden Bull*, climb a shallow corner.

5. Neutron Star 5.10a

The next corner right of the previous route.

6. Diet Of Worms 5.10a

Climb the crack in the corner of the huge block dihedral. Good but sometimes guano-covered.

7. Impossible Crack 5.10d

This is the striking fist and hand crack right of *Diet of Worms*. A big swing awaits a falling toproper.

NIP AND TUCK

Nip and Tuck is another of Boulder Canyon's drive-up climbing areas. The topropes listed are probably far enough from the road to accommodate children. 20-30 foot slings are helpful for the topropes.

1. Arete 5.10d
2. Antagonism 5.12a

Difficult face climbing.

3. Finger Crack 5.9

One of the finest crack climbs in the Boulder area!

CENOTAPH CRAG

Cenotaph is one of the westernmost of Boulder Canyon's crags. The cliff is impossible to see when driving up the canyon, so check your mileage, drive past the crag and turn around. It is easily visible on the hillside to the north when driving down. The most distinguishing feature is a prominent sharp arete at the crag's center. Despite quality rock, this crag is usually uncrowded.

Approach Cenotaph via a bushwhack from the road. The climbs begin from a large slabular ledge obtained via a short scramble. The top of the cliff is accessed via a chimney-gully system left of *Goin' Down In It*, or a longer walk around the left side. For this reason all routes have a difficult access. Each route on Cenotaph has its own anchor requirements; thus the icon is placed next to each route.

1. Goin' Down In It 5.9
Climb the center of the black streak. Gear and a wimpy tree serve as anchors. (20-35 ft. slings).

2. Ethereal 5.9
Crack right of black streak. Gear and tree anchors. (30-40 ft. slings).

3. Apparition 5.11a
Starts ten feet left of the arete and climbs cracks to the top three bolts. Bolt anchors.

4. Phantasm 5.11b/c
Climbs the bolted arete. Bolt anchors.

5. Right to Life 5.9+
The dihedral can be toproped. (30-40 ft. slings).

6. Phaedra 5.11c
The first route right of the dihedral. (This route and its two right-hand neighbors can be toproped via bolts and natural anchors, but bolts come and go on this crag, so bring long slings and you can arrange something).

7. Euphoria 5.11b
A line squeezed between its neighbors.

8. Up Above It 5.10
One bolt then right to a seam.

9. Unknown 5.8
Right of #8.

GREGORY CANYON AMPHITHEATER

The Gregory Canyon Amphitheater is one of the more popular and established toproping areas in Boulder. Many Front Range climbers cut their teeth on the routes of the West Bench. The area is very user friendly, save for the seasonal poison ivy found on the trails.

To reach the Amphitheater, take Baseline Road west from town and drive past Chautauqua Park. Look for a "Fire Danger" sign just as the road veers right to head up Flagstaff Mountain. Take the smaller road to the left across a bridge and continue to the trailhead at a cul-de-sac parking area. The Ampitheater Trail departs the lot to the south and crosses a foot bridge almost immediately. After about ten minutes of walking, a Climber Access trail signs denote the Amphiteater as well as trails to the anchor access.

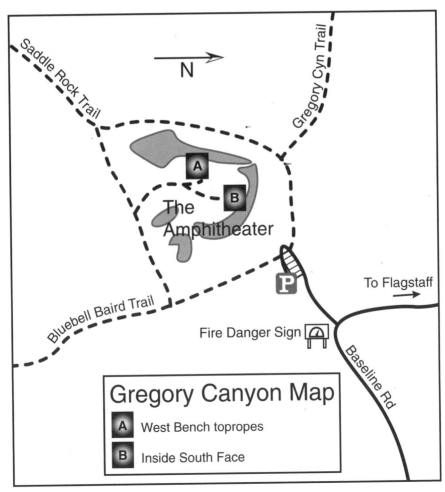

Gregory Canyon Map

A West Bench topropes

B Inside South Face

1. Inside South Face 5.10 - 5.11 ● ∅

As one peers into the Amphitheater from the trail, this is the climb that first comes into view. This is a wandering line, usually defined by an abundance of chalk. Though originally rated 5.9, most parties will feel that the climbing is a number grade harder. The bolts at the top require nearly 20 feet of extension to avoid rope wear and to allow a 50-meter cord to reach the ground. The best toprope is actually left of the bolts when looking at the wall from the ground. An airy 4th class approach from the west gains the anchors. 40-50 ft. slings.

2. West Bench Topropes 5.3 - 5.7 ◑ ▲ ∕

The West Bench is the lower-angled wall on the west end of the Amphitheater. Many routes and variations of routes make their way up this wall. The rightmost routes are easier, while the left-hand (southern) routes are more difficult. A lone Colorado Mountain Club bolt serves as an anchor for the left side routes (it can be backed up by a tunnel thread). The right-hand routes can be toproped by tying off boulders, placing gear, or (with enough sling) tying off a distant tree. Get to the top by following a trail just uphill from the Amphitheater. This approach is labeled "Climber Access". 20-50 ft. slings are needed for these routes.

FLAGSTAFF MOUNTAIN

Flagstaff Mountain has received a deserved popularity as a bouldering area, yet it also houses many excellent toprope problems — some with roadside access and some that are hidden gems nestled among the pines.

Mileage for the parking areas and climbs on Flagstaff are taken from the "Fire Danger" sign on Baseline Road.

Flagstaff Mountain is a fee area for non-residents of Boulder. If your automobile license plates do not signify Boulder registration, you must pay a fee to park on the mountain.

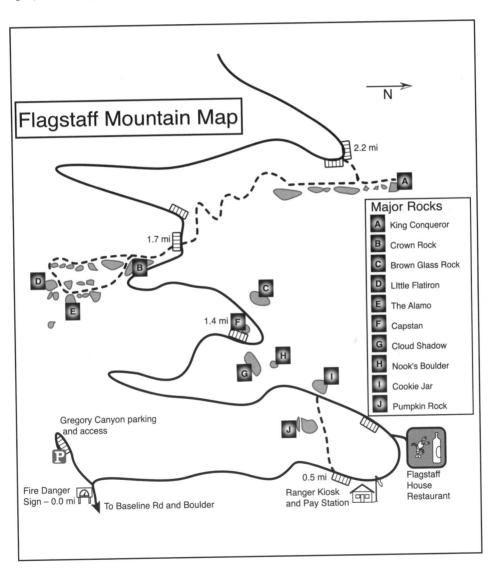

Flagstaff Mountain Map

N

2.2 mi

1.7 mi

1.4 mi

0.5 mi

Gregory Canyon parking and access

Fire Danger Sign – 0.0 mi

To Baseline Rd and Boulder

Ranger Kiosk and Pay Station

Flagstaff House Restaurant

Major Rocks

A	King Conqueror
B	Crown Rock
C	Brown Glass Rock
D	LIttle Flatiron
E	The Alamo
F	Capstan
G	Cloud Shadow
H	Nook's Boulder
I	Cookie Jar
J	Pumpkin Rock

PUMPKIN ROCK (5.11)

This prominent feature is located about a half mile from the Fire sign, near the Flagstaff House Restaurant. Park at the lot near the ranger kiosk and hike past bathrooms to the rock. Be on the lookout for poison ivy along the trail and near the base of the climbs. The climbs of interest ascend pin scars on the overhanging north face. Many variations exist; the most difficult ascends the pin scars in a straight-up line. CMC bolts are accessed via a ramp-like affair (one steep step) on the opposite side. These routes often stay dry on rainy days. Bring 10-20 foot slings.

THE COOKIE JAR (5.7-5.10)

Just up the road from Pumpkin Rock is The Cookie Jar. Park near the rock at 0.8 miles in a designated spot and make a short hike. The obvious wide crack is the main objective, but more difficult variations are possible. 10-20 foot slings are needed.

THE CAPSTAN (5.9-5.11)

This little pinnacle is located at the hairpin turn at mile 1.4. A pinnacle-like projection can be slung to create a toprope anchor; gain this via a boulder problem on the north side which leads to an easier scramble. Problems are on the south and west walls and can be modified to include any number of difficulties. The obvious pin scarred finger crack probably clocks in at 5.11. The face left of this can be navigated in a variety of fashions ranging from hard 5.9 to hard 5.11. Bring 10-20 foot slings.

Cloud Shadow Wall (5.10-5.11)

Park at The Capstan, but hike on the road to the guardrail at the hairpin turn. A trail leads to the Cloud Shadow Wall which can be toproped at many places. Old quarter-inch bolts mark the best sites for anchors, though only one is still usable (and serves as an anchor for *Concentration*, a difficult 5.11 problem). Never rely on a single quarter-inch bolt!

Nook's Rock (5.7-5.9)

This boulder offers some of the finest moderate toproping on Flagstaff. Most of the routes are between 5.7 and 5.9 in difficulty. Unfortunately getting to the bolts on the summit is almost as difficult as the routes. Access the crag by hopping over the guardrail uphill from the Cloud Shadow approach and descending a gully/trail to the East/NE until this large boulder comes into view. It is easily identified by the trees abutting the rock. The easiest summit route is via the NW corner in a dish near a leaning pine. Bring 5-10 foot slings.

CROWN ROCK

Crown Rock is the prominent rock that marks the main bouldering area of Flagstaff. Park at the paved parking area and approach from here. The most common topropes are found on the slabby east face. The conundrum, however, is this: getting to the top to set up anchors is at least as difficult as the climbs. If, however, you're looking for an excellent spot to take beginners, this is it. The approach is nil as the rock essentially backs up to the road. While this is great for small children as far as the walk is concerned, you'll want to watch them given the proximity to traffic. Access to the top is via a steep scramble on the south edge.

East Face Topropes (5.2-5.6)

The east face of Crown Rock is a popular teaching area. The climbing is similar to that on the Third Flatiron, though difficult variations can be found.

Katelyn Benton on Crown Rock

LITTLE FLATIRON (5.9-5.10)

This crag is approached by hiking south from the paved parking lot at mile 1.7. Continue past the Monkey Traverse boulder problem until the rock comes into view. A tree very near the edge of the crag's summit and a ledge at 3/4 height marks this route.

THE ALAMO

The next Flatiron-like feature uphill and southeast of The Little Flatiron is The Alamo. It is easily recognized as the highest point on the hill — a Flatiron-like rock with a wide crack on the right. Approach the anchors via the low-angle analog crack on the back side; you might want to shoe-up for the scramble.

1. Remember The Alamo 5.10d

This is the premier wide-crack toprope. Popular and difficult.

KING CONQUEROR

The K.C. Boulder can be approached from the Crown Rock parking area or by driving to another parking spot at mile 2.2. This formation is the northernmost rock of interest to climbers. From the latter parking area descend downhill to the main trail, then north to an obvious boulder marked by a large pipe rising from its summit. This can be used for an anchor.

1. King Conqueror 5.11

A classic line that recently got harder after a key hold broke. Bring 10-20 ft. slings to toprope this hand-crack test piece.

Note: Next crack to the lft of King Conqueror is 5.10-, and the arete to the right K.C. is 5.10.

THE FLATIRONS

The skyline west of Boulder is home to some of the area's best moderate climbing, but like Eldorado Canyon, the size of most of the formations hinders their accessibility for toproping. Some outstanding exceptions exist; the bulk of which are covered in the Flagstaff Mountain section. The rest will be described north to south in this section.

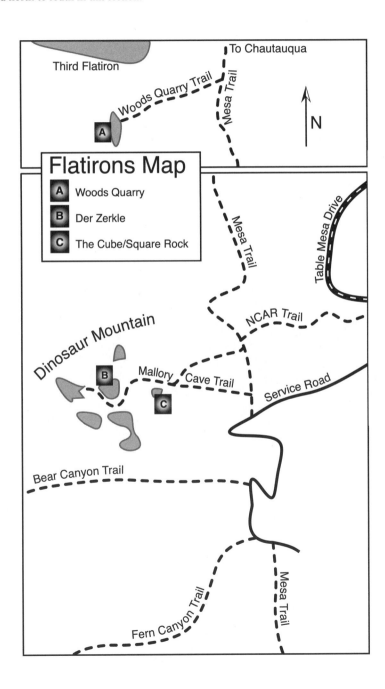

WOODS QUARRY

This long-abandoned quarry offers a degree of solitude and some excellent friction climbing in the 5.8 to easy 5.10 range. The wall's 65 degree angle tests the footwork of experienced climbers, while allowing advanced beginners to feel comfortable. Woods Quarry is easily viewed from Broadway, as it lies just above the Mesa Trail between NCAR and Chautauqua Park. Though many approaches are possible, the easiest is via the Woods Quarry Trail, a variant of the Mesa Trail as one leaves Chautauqua.

Access to the top of the crag is gained by a trail that is found at the junction of the quarry's northern terminus and the main hiking trail. The start of the trail is difficult to locate, but can be found by walking under the large tree where rocks are laid out in the diagram of an unfinished rectangle. The top of the cliff contains a fair bit of loose scree and some down-climbing is required to get to the tree anchors for toproping, so use great caution if others are below. 30-40 ft. slings are a must, as the wall is often higher than 80 feet. An additional 10-20 foot extension can also eliminate climbing loose rock up high. The base of the crag is unsuitable for small children as it contains loose talus and some poison ivy. However, the Mesa Trail is OK for kids.

1. Non-Friction 5.8

This ascends the left side past four old bolts.

2. The Middle Way 5.9

A nondescript line right of *Non-Friction*.

3. Diatribe 5.10a

This climbs the small but obvious seam that once offered bolt protection.

4. Quarry Wall 5.8

The four-bolt route on the right that sports a two-bolt anchor. These 1/4 inch bolts, however, might best serve as a directional which can be clipped by a slight pendulum from the tree anchor above *Diatribe*.

5. Don't Stop Now 5.9

This climbs the crack on the right.

Square Rock/The Cube

This brilliant formation located a short ways up the Mallory Cave Trail is the home of many good, although difficult, toprope problems. Approach by hiking from NCAR to the Mesa Trail, then hike a short distance south to the Mallory Cave Trail, and follow that trail west until the obvious square-shaped rock comes into view.

The summit sports an array of bolts that were placed with little regard as to optimal toproping location, so long slings (20-30 ft.) are a must for most routes. The top of The Cube is accessed by a tree-climb on the northwest corner. (Without the tree this route goes at 5.8.)

1. Flake 5.10
The right-facing flake on the SE side.

2. Crack 5.11c
A steep crack 5 feet right of the previous route.

3. Android Powerpack 5.12d/13a
Start in the middle of the east face at a left-facing flake. Head left at a small roof, then follow a shallow right facing corner to the top.

4. Yellow Christ 5.12b
Start up the same flake as #3. Stay right where *Android* heads left, following a left-facing corner to the top.

5. Stoic Buttress 5.11c
On the NE side, climb a short crack, head right towards its top, then back left over delicate face moves.

DER ZERKLE

1. What If You're Not 5.8

A fun route that is located about five to ten minutes uphill from The Cube, and almost directly above the Mallory Cave Trail. It is found by continuing 50 feet past the point where the trail makes a sharp left. Step past a short retaining wall of piled rocks and look for a huecoed route with four bolts to the right. Two more difficult bolted routes are located directly above the trail as well. One can scramble around left to reach the bolt anchors to set up a toprope. The wall on either side can be toproped from gear. These outings are about the same grade.

COUCH POTATO

The Couch Potato is a large boulder located beneath the hogback ridge that runs south to north beginning near Eldorado Springs. Hike along the Old South Mesa Trail, then cross-country to the crag. Excellent rock and a steep technical face climbing make this one of the best hard toprope problems.

1. Sofa Patrol 5.12a
Climbs the center of the face.
2. Couch Potato 5.12b
A more difficult dynamic problem to the right.

ELDORADO CANYON

Upon entry it becomes obvious that Eldorado Canyon is limited as a toproping area; the size of the walls is a detriment. Nonetheless, Eldorado is the home of many toprope problems.

Approach Eldorado Canyon by exiting Boulder via south-bound Highway 93 (Broadway). At the first traffic signal outside the city limits, hang a right. Follow the road past the pavement into the canyon. Eldo is a State Park requiring an entrance fee of $4.00/vehicle, $1.00 for walk-in, or $40.00 annual.

The vast size and unusual layout of Eldorado Canyon make it difficult to describe access to the many topropeable pitches. This guide will cover those that are easily accessed, but will not include other pitches that may be toproped but are difficult to locate or reside in distant singular locations.

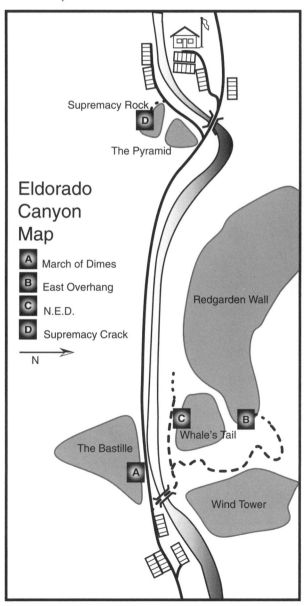

Eldorado
Canyon
Map

A March of Dimes

B East Overhang

C N.E.D.

D Supremacy Crack

N

THE BASTILLE

The first routes you will encounter on The Bastille (the large cliff on the left as one enters Eldorado Canyon) are on the March of Dimes Buttress. To get to the anchors, climb a ramp that begins about 80 meters left of the start of the route. Traverse along the top of a broken buttress to reach the bolts. Short slings needed (10-25 ft).

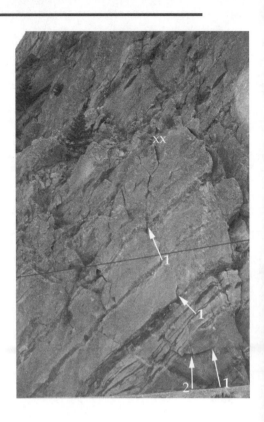

1. March of Dimes 5.9
The right-hand crack first pitch can be toproped.
2. Variation 5.10d
Climb the left-hand crack for the first 15 feet.
3. Lilliburlero 5.12a
The rightmost line on the March of Dimes Buttress. Climb a thin right-angling crack.

REDGARDEN WALL

This is the biggest wall in Eldorado Canyon but the topropes are found at its eastern terminus just above the Wind Tower Trail. Approach the *East Overhang* by crossing the bridge and following the first steep trail that meanders steeply upwards towards the Wind Tower. The toprope problem is visible the entire time.

1. The East Overhang 5.10-5.11

A short, dark, overhanging, and huecoed wall is encountered at a point where the Wind Tower Trail more or less dead ends at a chockstone. To get to the top scramble through shrubberies and weeds to a ramp which is climbed past pines and junipers to the top of the route. 30-40 foot slings are a must. Some people sling the giant flake; others place gear. The center line is 5.10, and left of center is more difficult.

THE WHALE'S TAIL

This formation is encountered on the north side of the creek and houses some interesting topropes, though none in the moderate grades. Most anchors are difficult to get to or require leading an easier route. The following routes are included because they are frequently climbed, but I don't recommend them for inexperienced climbers as the anchors aren't easily reached (5-10 foot slings).

1. N.E.D. 5.12b
The big roof left of the cave.

2. Johnny Belinda 5.12c
The slimy jugs and crack along the cave's right edge.

3. Amputee Love 5.12d
A short hard problem named for Hugh Herr.

4. Bowling For Tourists 5.11
Named after the results of a fall.

SUPREMACY ROCK

This is the quartzite outcropping near the visitor center at the western end of the canyon. Drive up the road to the upper picnic area but don't cross the bridge. Park at one of the obvious lots near the crag. Supremacy proper is the big rock with a slabby north face and steep south face. The summit is gained by a scramble up the east side.

North Face Routes

1. Northeast Arete 5.7
As the name implies.

2. Supremacy Slab 5.9
This outing starts left of the fir tree and climbs a groove, joining the arete near its top. Harder variations abound on either side

3. Overhanging Arete 5.9
This ascends the left side of the arete on the western end of the north face.

South Face Routes

4. Supremacy Crack 5.11b

This can be toproped, though its angle requires directionals to prevent a falling climber from taking the king swing.

5. The Web 5.13b

Could be toproped, but why?

THE PYRAMID

This is the rock just below the previous routes. From the west, an obvious pyramid is visible. The tree works fine as the main anchor, but be sure to set up directionals with gear. Bring 20-40 foot slings.

1. Simple Simon Slab 5.6

Start right of a tree and ascend a crack.

2. Northwest Arete 5.8+

Climb the arete formed by the intersection of the north face and the triangle wall.

3. West Face 5.10a

This ascends the difficult triangular face for which The Pyramid is named.

Fran Bagenal on Politicians, Priests, and Body Bags.
Photo by Steve "Crusher" Bartlett

GOLDEN AREA

A decade ago no one would have thought of going to Golden to climb. With the advent of sport climbing at North Table Mountain, however, came a shift in climbing's conventional wisdom. The broken basalt crags overlooking the Coors Brewery have received deserved popularity, a result largely of the concentration of moderate routes — an anomaly among Front Range sport crags.

Table Mountain is also an ideal toproping area. Its easternmost cliffs offer easy access to bolt anchors, and on a spring or fall weekend it isn't uncommon to find half the parties toproping. Summer months can be hot on the primarily south-facing cliffs, though ambitious chameleons can run for sun. For the other nine months, Table is a welcomed retreat from the rock gyms. This guide lists the most popular toprope climbs, though many more lines can be toproped. Mark Rolofson's comprehensive guide is a good resource.

Much thanks should be given to the Access Fund for acquiring the land amid access troubles.

While Table Mountain may be the most popular area near Golden, the Lookout Mountain Crag provides a brief escape into the world of quality granite climbing. Reminiscent of Yosemite granite, this small cliff offers crack and face climbs on a steep slab.

Golden is experiencing a virtual renaissance. Take some time to check out the revitalised downtown area: visit the American Mountain Club Library, drink some coffee, chat with Greg at the Bent Gate, grab a meal. Have a golden time.

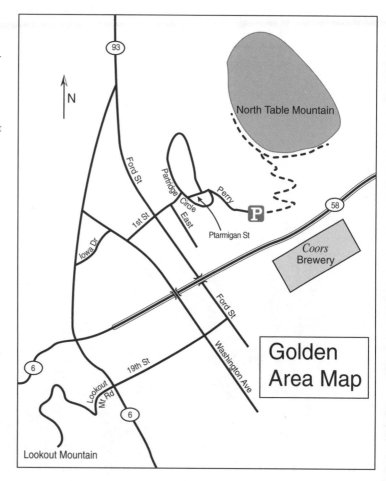

NORTH TABLE MOUNTAIN

North Table Mountain is a popular sport climbing area near Golden offering a scenic bird's eye view of the Coors Brewery. The basalt cliffs are not only conducive to, but are also popular for, toproping. While the majority of routes have been established as sport leads, the climbs on the right side are popular for toproping and are the routes identified in this guide.

Please use the new designated parking areas and approach trails. Two parking lots now serve climbers and hikers; there is no need to park on the residential streets. Routes in this guide are identified from right to left as they are encountered on the approach.

The following symbols are applicable for all of the routes on North Table Mountain. All routes have bolt anchors. Gear could be an asset for those occasional awkward reaches.

Cammie Muller enjoying Table Mountain.
Photo by Steve Muller.

North Table Mountain

North Table Mountain routes are described from right to left as they are encountered along the approach

1. Louise 5.8

This route climbs a bolted crack to the summit of a micro-tower. Three bolts with gold-shut anchors.

2. Thelma 5.7

The tower's arete. Same anchors as *Louise*.

3. Kid's Climb 5.9+

Climb a rounded tower. The first hanger was missing at press time.

4. New River Gorge Homesick Blues 5.11b/c

Climb in from the right to join a smooth slender face. Three bolts.

5. The Virus 5.12a

The bolted face right of a groove. The crux is down low.

6. Thick Crust 5.7

The wide groove.

7. Unnamed Face 5.11

The clean face left of *Stemming Wide*.

8. Stemming Wide 5.8

The aesthetic stemming corner.

9. Old Roof Route 5.8

Excellent climb on holds from buckets to crimps.

10. Protection From the Virus 5.10c

The *Old Roof's* lefthand neighbor.

11. Interface 5.8

A clean albeit short face route. The bolt anchors are a long reach below the summit.

12. Tenacious 5.10a

Climb to the ledge at 1/3 height then wander up a streak.

13. Jolobee 5.11b/c
Scramble to the base of a clean face then proceed up the short cruxy wall.
14. Bullet the Brown Cloud 5.11a/b
The knife-edge arete.
15. 5.6 Crack 5.6
16. Deck Chairs on the Titanic 5.9+
One of Table's best routes.
17. New Route 5.8
A broken wandering route.
18. Another New Route 5.10d
The route between a chimney and perfect hand crack. The crack is a good 5.8, but is not marked on the photo.
19. Brown Cloud Arete 5.10
The route on the far left of the alcove.

Steuart Green photo

20. Unknown 5.7

This route and its neighbor offer quality climbing, but the anchors are difficult to reach for toproping. Perhaps an anchor could be arranged off gear.

21. Unknown 5.8

22. Fabulous Flying Carr's Route 5.11a

Begin up a slender spire and finish on the clean face. This photo is taken from an awkward angle.

23. This Ain't Naturita, Pilgrim 5.9

Considered a classic, this climbs a nice prow with a sharpish arete. The anchors are difficult to access.

24. Smear Me A Beer 5.11b

Climb a slender spire, then finish on a blunt arete.

25. Mrs. Hen Lays A Peck 5.12a

This difficult clean climb can be toproped by swinging from the anchors on the *Unknown Arete* and clipping the anchors as directionals. Starts left of a hole.

26. Unknown Arete 5.11c

A devious arete/crack/weird line left of *Mrs. Hen*. Shares *Mrs. Hen's* start and is also difficult to toprope from the bolt anchors.

27. Here Today, Gone Tomorrow 5.9 or 5.11d

Like so many climbing legends... The boulder problem at the first bolt adds much difficulty.

28. Handle This Hard On 5.12a

This 5-bolt line would be difficult to toprope.

29. Tora, Tora, Tora 5.11b/c

Climb a corner to a short, steep face.

30. Mr. Squirrel Places A Nut 5.11c

The big roof.

31. In Between the Lines 5.9-

Around the corner from *Mr. Squirrel* are three routes. This is the rightmost.

32. Unknown 5.9

A newish route just left of #31. Begin up a slender rib of rock then step right to another rib.

33. Unknown 5.8

Climb a face, step left and head past bolts to a ledge. Be cautious setting up this toprope.

34. Beer Barrel Buttress 5.10d

Climb to the top of a small pillar, then continue up an ever-widening expanse of rock.

35. The Ground Doesn't Lie 5.10c/d

Yet we lie on the ground. Use caution when scrambling down to the anchors on this route.

THE INDUSTRIAL BUTTRESS

After an expanse of routes on considerably broken rock, the basalt again becomes smoother and aesthetic. To reach the quality routes of the Industrial Buttress continue past the barbed wire fence for a hundred meters or so. The buttress is located just past an obvious talus-strewn slope that affords access to the anchors.

36. Table Manners 5.11c

Something absent at Cafe Gondolier all-you-can-eat pasta nights. A difficult thin face that tackles roofs up high.

37. Shadow of a Hangdog 5.10b

Certainly the prettiest crack climb at Table Mountain. This climb faces SE.

38. Brain Cloud 5.9

The quality arete.

39. Major Bolt Achievement 5.11a/b

Start up the face and finish through a roof.

40. Shark Attack 5.10d

Sink your teeth into this one. Start this route the same as for the following climb, however finish right up the crack instead of chasing bolts. Set up a separate anchor.

41. Feeding Frenzy 5.11d

Another route name with an all-you-can-eat theme. Begin up a face and continue via technical stemming. This climb faces SW.

Stewart Green photo

Stewart Green photo

42. Industrial Disease 5.11c
Some call this Table's best route. Follow a tips crack to a crux bulge.

43. Flight 67 5.11a
Begin left of *Industrial Disease* and climb the left side of the bulge.

44. Take Flight 5.9 or 5.11c
A contrived boulder problem start can make this a significantly harder route.

45. Salad Bar 5.10a
This tasty route climbs a steep face with four bolts.

46. Fast Boat to China 5.8
A crack in a corner system.

47. Politicians, Priests, and Body Bags 5.10a
A short crack leads to a ledge and then the face above.

48. Heidi Hi 5.8
A left-facing corner system shares anchors with *Politicians*.

Helpful Hint:
While most of the bolt anchors at Table Mountain can be reached from the top of the cliff, it is still a wise idea to carry some long slings and a few pieces of pro. You might find a route or two that requires them or an anchor or two you wouldn't want to scramble to.

Lookout Mountain Crag

The Lookout Mountain Crag, just above Golden, is the home of several fantastic routes on an impeccable steep granite slab. Turn off Highway 6 on Lookout Mountain Road (19th St.). Follow this for 1.8 miles to a pullout on the right side. A trail leads east of the parking area and down to the cliffs. The short final scramble might prove a detriment to smaller children. Bring long slings and some gear. The bolt anchors are practically useless for toproping as they are well beneath the top.

1. 5.7 Crack
The prominent left-facing dihedral.
2. 5.8 Crack
3. Face Route 5.10a
Climb up and over a roof passing a couple of bolts.
4. 5.9+ Crack
5. Face Route #2 5.9
Another bolted face line that makes a great toprope.
6. 5.8 Crack
The crack line left of the serrated left-facing corner.

Scott Arledge on Hippopromis

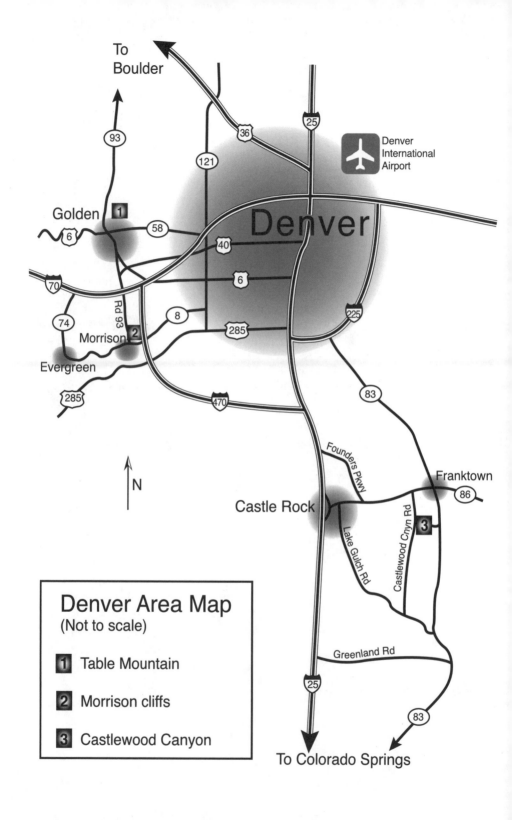

DENVER METRO AREA

The Mile High City, home of the Broncos, the Avalanche, the Rockies, and the well — uh Nuggets, is quite the sporting town. Amid all this throwing, catching, drooling, and fighting ("I went to a fight and a hockey game broke out") Denver offers much in the way of real sports. Ernest Hemingway once penned something to the effect that "there are only three sports: mountain climbing, motor racing, and bull fighting. The rest are merely games."

Denver is conveniently situated in the center of more climbing areas than you can shake a stick at. Lets face it, many of the crags in this book could be considered part of the greater Denver area, but we snooty Boulderites like to think of most of them as ours. As a show of good faith, though, we'll concede the best and easternmost of the toproping areas to Denver. Castlewood Canyon, located east of I-25 near Castle Rock, is the metro area's hidden gem. The canyon contains more easily-toproped routes than any other area in the state. Top it off with quality rock and enough facets to ensure year-round cragging, and Castlewood becomes a true destination area.

Another priceless Denver area is the bouldering mecca of Morrison cliffs. I've said it about a million times and probably even meant it a few — Morrison is the best crag in the world. O.K., so I said it mostly when I've been in a bouldering tizzy. If Morrison had more than a couple of topropes, it would also be an amazing climbing area. Still, the existing lines are so good that the area is worth a visit if just for the afternoon. Besides, the pastries at the nearby bakery are reason enough to make the drive (from say Kansas, even).

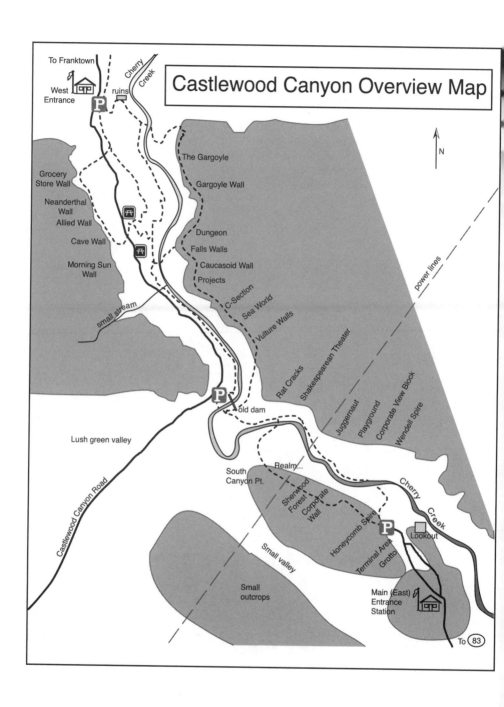

Castlewood Canyon Overview Map

CASTLEWOOD CANYON

Castlewood Canyon, the easternmost of Colorado's climbing areas is perhaps the best toproping area in the Front Range. The area is home to over 300 routes, the vast majority of which are toprope problems. Approaches vary from exceptionally mellow to half hour bushwacks, while the canyon's various aspects allow for year-round climbing.

Turning east off I-25 might seem odd for rockclimbers, but Castlewood is worth the visit. In fact, it might become addicting. The region gets more rain than Denver, yet it seems to be a blend of high desert and lush forest. The canyon's rim is reminiscent of the Colorado Plateau, generally barren excepting scrub oak, Ponderosa pines, and Gambel oaks. Inside the canyon, Cherry Creek passes through pine and aspen forests, sandy beaches, and clay walls.

The 25 million-year-old Castlewood Conglomerate, the unique sedimentary rock that forms the cliffs and boulders, provides a plethora of climbing options which include pockets, edges, cracks, and knobs. The routes are generally short and toprope anchors are fairly accessible. Some cliffs, such as the Grocery Store Wall, are littered with bolt anchors and toprope problems. Other walls contain sport routes, but almost always the anchors are close enough to the rim to be accessed with a careful reach. Long slings are sometimes needed to tie off trees or natural anchors; a few routes require gear; most climbs, though, can be toproped from bolts.

Though Castlewood is Colorado's best toprope area and is nearly perfect for kids, be aware that some walls are crowded with ropes constantly flying off the top, that some of the rock is questionable, and that a rattlesnake danger exists.

The main canyon is reached by turning off I-25 at Castle Rock (Exit 182) if coming from the south. From Denver it is quicker to turn off at Exit 184 (by the outlet stores) and follow Founder's Parkway to the intersection with Highway 86). 5.7 miles from the 182 exit (0.25 miles west of Franktown) a sign indicates Castlewood Canyon Road. Follow this gravel road for 2.0 miles to the park's westernmost entrance and the first areas covered in this book.

To reach the Inner Canyon and the East entrance, continue on 86 to Franktown, turn south on Highway 83 and follow signs to Castlewood Canyon's East Entrance, home of the Visitor Center and large picnic areas. Alternatively, from Colorado Springs, one can follow the winding Highway 83 to the entrance.

Castlewood Canyon, like most State Parks, requires a daily use fee of $4.00 or a State Park annual pass (the same as Eldorado Canyon).

Additional note: Castlewood Canyon is considered by many to be the best cool-weather bouldering area in the state. Phillip Benningfield's *Colorado Bouldering*, provides a vast amount of information on the park's boulders.

THE CAVE WALL

The Cave Wall is a great starting point for referencing routes on the western walls of the main canyon. The short approach and quality rock make this an excellent toprope area. The parking area and trail are clearly labeled along the road. The Cave itself can be explored from above. The top is accessed by an obvious scramble on the wall's right side. See photo for further information.

1. The Good, the Bad, and the Dirty 5.10d

The classic crack climb. Expect a crux at each bulge. Gear anchors.

2. Territorial Pissings 5.11b

Start about eight feet right of the huge block. Climb up the thin face on orange and green rock (30' slings).

3. Time Passages 5.10d/5.11a

Follow a thin crack to a face with a bolt. This marks the crux (30 ft. slings).

4. Hourglass Flake 5.11a

Don't bother (30 ft. slings).

5. Unknown 5.10d

A lone bolt defines this route near the descent route (30 ft. slings).

ALLIED WALL

The Allied Wall is approached via the Cave Wall Trail. Head right where the trail forks, rather than heading for the cave. The top is most easily accessed via the Cave Wall scramble.

Lauren Chelbowski on Hourglass Crack 5.11a. Photo: Dan Hare

1. Coalition 5.10a

Head straight up from the arching crack. Look for camouflaged anchor bolts right on the edge.

2. Allies 5.11

This route climbs the face to the right of *Coalition* via pockets. Long slings and/or gear.

3. Left Crack 5.11a

The lefthand arching crack can be toproped off a natural tunnel-thread, but to avoid a pendulum, you'd best toprope #4 first and place directionals on the way down.

4. Right Crack 5.10

The previous route's right-hand neighbor.

5. The Rock Rat 5.11a

This route is found right of the arching cracks. A one-bolt anchor is lacking a hanger.

THE NEANDERTHAL WALLS

This is a broad area between the Allied Walls and the Grocery Store Walls. For the sake of reference, the routes will be addressed as though you're coming from left to right — from the Allied Wall. A prominent feature and excellent reference point is Primal Jam, the heinous roof crack.

1. Mobious Strip 5.12a

The first route right of *The Rock Rat*. Located around the corner on a north-facing wall. Pebbles and large pockets lead to a bulge.

2. The Mosh 5.9

Offwidth to wide hands.

3. Outer Mongolia 5.10a

The north-facing section immediately right of *The Mosh*. Face climbing leads to left-facing dihedrals.

4. Primal Jam 5.11c

Makes for a better reference point than a toprope, but if you don't mind a swing....

5. The Way Out 5.7

As the name implies, this is the way out if you're stuck between the *Primal Jam* and *Rotunda*. Big flakes makes this not such an appealing route.

6. The Rotunda 5.10

The prominent steep east-facing wall right of *Primal Jam*. Finish on the arete's left side. Bolt anchors.

7. The Grind 5.11c

Continue down the trail about 33 paces past *The Rotunda* to a short arete that finishes on the north- facing wall.

8. Cheater Five 5.11a/b

The mossy dihedral with some old fixed pins.

9. Landlubber 5.10d

You could lub dis woot, even if you hated *Cheeter Five*. Head up the face right of #8, pass the small roof on its left side, and head toward the left side of the face.

10. Monopoly 5.11a

The tree up top has a monopoly on the anchor possibilities. Climb the wall between #9 and #11.

11. Husker Do? 5.11a

That is the question. The rightmost route on this clean east-facing wall. Gear, dear.

12. Adajam 5.5

Evejam's mate in the Old Testamant. The lefthand route that begins in the depression (25 ft. slings).

12a. Are You Experienced? 5.6

You could learn something from this wide crack. Start in the depression left of a detached block (25 ft. slings).

13. Where's the Jam? 5.11c

You'll ponder this question when the crack runs out. Look left and you'll find a hole instead. Gear makes the best anchor.

14. Pack the Walls 5.5

Follow double cracks on the north facing wall, immediately left of the Candyland Block. Gear, I fear.

15. The Fingers Have It 5.7+

The thin crack right of #14. Gear anchors.

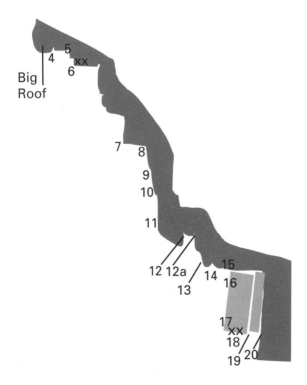

16. Candyland 5.10 or 5.11a

This is the route that takes the left side of the east face of the giant block. (Anchor requires 40 ft. slings tied to trees on the main cliff).

17. Stratego 5.11d/12a

The difficult route on the right side of the Candyland Block's east face. Ditto #16 on the anchor.

18. Stupid Manufactured Route A1

I give all artificial climbs the aid rating they deserve. Bolts beneath the summit.

19. Chicken Wing Crack 5.10

A wide crack on the left side of the pillar found between the block and the wall to its right. Anchors au naturel.

20. The Squeeze 5.11

The chimney turned offwidth at the entrance to the block's roundabout passage — a journey popular with hikers.

21. Cro-Mag Crack 5.10d

An prehistoric addictive substance. The first route on the long east-facing wall (20 ft. slings from a tree).

22. Wall of Webs 5.10b

Just right of #21, this route wanders about to a dished out section, then back again (20 ft. sling-o-ramas).

23. Parcheezee 5.11a

This and the next two routes climb the wall that sits above some large boulders. Find the volleyball-sized hole at the center of the wall. Start a little to the right. You'll need gear or long slings for the anchor.

24. Yahtzee 5.10d

Stay left of the dark streak, aiming for a thin crack above the recess (40 ft. slings).

25. Up the Red 5.10d

This route wanders about on the right-hand margin of the wall. The route-finding feels like you're up the Red without a paddle. Gear.

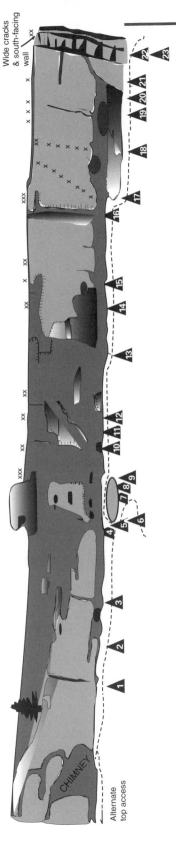

Wide cracks & south-facing wall

CHIMNEY

Alternate top access

THE GROCERY STORE WALL

The Grocery Store Wall is the best single toproping cliff in Castlewood Canyon. An abundance of bolt anchors, a high concentration of routes, and a mellow approach add up to pure fun. The best approach is to park at the first lot on the left as you're driving into the canyon. The trail and parking area are labeled with a "Climber's Trail" sign. The trail hits the wall at a grouping of routes in the area of *Hot Fudge* and its many variants. Getting to the top of the wall isn't like cruising down the isle at King Soops. Some possible fourth-class scrambles are found on the wall's left side, and if you head north enough, you can just walk up. Once you're up, though, you can keep switching the rope around.

The Grocery Store Wall

1. Hot Tuna 5.9+
Climb some pockets to gain a crack. Ends at a big ledge (50 ft. slings). Not pictured.

2. Hamburger Helper 5.10
Start out at a small cave and end at a depression on the ledge. Not pictured.

3. Hamburger 5.10
The finger and hand crack. If you don't want to hamburger your hands, try taping. Double bolts. Not pictured.

4. Cactus Flower 5.10a
Things get a little tight with the next few routes. Climb left of the arete (50 ft. slings or gear).

5. Shake & Bake 5.11
The arete left of the turd offwidth.

6. Petrified Turd 5.8
A guano-filled wide crack, as classic as the name.

7. Donut Hole 5.11
A classic route that powers out *Hot Fudge's* undercling roof to gain the big hole.

8. Hot Fudge 5.8
The classic undercling with big pendulum potential.

9. Fudge Face 5.10
Start left of the boulder and climbs the clean face right of *Hot Fudge*.

10. Peaches and Scream 5.7
Climbs up to the obvious flake and continues right via ledges and the like.

11. Zucchini 5.5
A right-angling crack system. Probably better as a lead. A directional will eliminate a humungous swing.

12. Peppermint Patty 5.11c
Starts off the small ledge a few feet off the ground and climbs the difficult wall above.

13. Rats Nest 5.8
A very thin crack pierces a hole and aims for a three-bolt anchor.

14. Pretzel Logic 5.11c
Begin at a roof about five feet above the ground, climbing up to and around the right side of the hole, then aim left.

15. You Name It 5.12a
Climb out of the black roof near a thin seam. The toprope bolts are hard to spot as they're just over the edge.

16. Licorice Stick 5.9
The left-leaning crack in the dark corner.

17. Gatoraide 5.12d
The recently rebolted test piece.

18. Boxo No No 5.11a

This sport route can be toproped from bolts beneath the summit. One of Castlewood's finest routes.

19. Rain Dance Crack 5.10a

The crack right of *Boxo*. When the crack ends, the face dance begins.

20. Rain Dance 5.9+

Paralleling the crack is a face route. The various bolts can all be used to back each other up.

21. Frosted Flakes 5.10+

The route right of *Rain Dance*. Terrrrrific!

22. Carmel Corner 5.5

The ledgy corner can be TR'd from a tunnel thread.

Melissa Lester on Rain Dance Crack

23. Carmel Corner Layback 5.5
24. Blood Pudding 5.9+
Climb the center of the south facing wall.
Bolt anchors.

25. Unknown
Bolt anchors. Not pictured

26. The Scoop 5.11
Find a water trough with a single bolt about a third of
the way up. Tree anchors.

27. Teething Biscuit 5.10
The route just right of #25, identified by a mail-slot
hueco. Bolt anchors just below the top.

28. Banana Split Chimney 5.4
Just left of the Banana Tower.

29. Banana Peel 5.8
The left-hand route on the east face of Banana Tower.
Bolts on top serve as anchors for the next three climbs.
A tricky step is required to reach the top.

30. Banana Shake 5.9
The right-hand face route on the tower.

31. Banana Flip 5.6
Takes the north ridge of Banana Tower.

The Banana Tower, Grocery Store Wall

GROCERY STORE WALL, NORTHERN TERMINUS

The following short, yet quality, routes are reached by walking a couple hundred yards to the terminus of the Grocery Store Wall. Routes 32 and 33 face east; the others are north facing. The northern routes can be identified by their division into three distinct faces. The top is accessed by the chimney with the dead tree (just right of the climbs) or by walking a little further west to a very easy scramble. The climbs take advantage of old Star-drive bolts so be cautious. Long slings are needed to back up one bolt to another, or to use trees as back-ups.

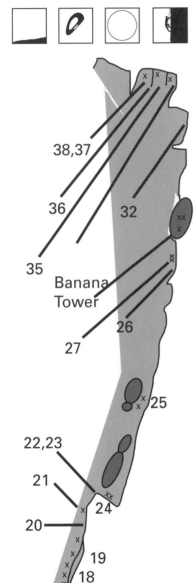

32. The Arledge Route 5.9 or 5.9+
This short toprope has two variants. Climbing right of the anchor pictured is harder than staying to the left. Big cams for anchors.

33. Rainbow Bread 5.9+
On the last east-facing wall are two climbs. Wander around the center of the face. Gear or long slings are helpful.

34. Pecan Pie 5.8-
Same start as #32, but angle right to the arete.

35. Pie in the Sky 5.10d
Start near the left arete of the center face and climb to the top, moving toward the center. Back up the Star-drive bolt.

36. Strawberry Jam 5.5
The offwidth crack that divides the middle and right-hand walls.

37. Gorilla Milk Direct 5.9
Climb the center of the right wall.

38. Gorilla Milk 5.7+
This route climbs the right-hand side of the right face.

Katelyn Benton on Rainbow Bread

THE FALLS WALL

The Falls Wall is the main climbing area in Castlewood Canyon. The highest concentration of quality routes lie between the Falls Wall and the southern terminus of the East Rim. Many of the climbs have been established as leads, though most can be toproped. For the sake of orientation, I've included all routes; textual descriptions will indicate if a climb cannot be toproped.

Approach from the Falls Trail which spurs off the Creek Bottom Trail. Park at the last available parking area on the left before the road narrows. The area is easily identified by its location directly above the waterfalls and the concentration of large boulders along the base.

A. Bridge of Sighs 5.9
Climb the far right side of the Block's north face.

B. Confederate 5.13a
Climb the left-hand edge of the west face.

C. Bolt Route 5.12b
The bolt route can be toproped.

1. Gonzo 5.11d
Of course the miniature flatiron's steep side has been toproped. Tie off the entire summit for an anchor.

2. Swinging Sirloin 5.11c
This excellent four-bolt sport route can be toproped from its bolt anchors.

3. Small Feat 5.10

The south-facing prow left of a chimney and right of *Swinging Sirloin* houses some interesting face climbing.

4. Out of Arm's Reach 5.10b

This is the leftmost of three sport routes. Begin behind a tree. You'll need gear for an anchor.

5. Tendon Terror 5.12a

A contrived but difficult toprope between routes #4 and #6.

6. Arborist Arms 5.11a

The middle bolted line with bolt anchors.

7. Invaders From the North 5.11b/c

A tricky climb that follows bolts around an arching corner.

8. Bitch 5.10

If you need Vedauwoo practice struggle up this teething offwidth. The sturdy but dead tree could be avoided as an anchor if you've brought some gear.

9. Steam Rock Fever 5.8-

The beautiful corner right of *Bitch*.

10. The Fat Raisin Sings 5.11b

Climb between the arete and route #11. (B.Y.O.A. : Bring Your Own Anchors).

12. Not Long For This World 5.10

A fantastic route up a shallow right-facing corner. Bolts at the top.

13. Internal Affairs 5.11b

A tricky face climb right of *Not Long....* Avoid the corner to the right. This route is best toproped from gear in the highest tier of rock; you could also risk the swing from #12's anchors.

14. It's Flakey 5.7

Like a good croissant. Climb the twin cracks in the main inside corner.

The author, doing some research on the Falls Wall

15. Chimney Sweep 5.5
A beautiful chimney worthy of the Canyonlands.

16. Elliott and the Flying Tsetses 5.10
Climb the wall about 10 feet right of the chimney (20-30 ft. slings gain trees).

17. Abo 5.11
Same long sling situation.

18. Blue Event Horizon 5.12c
A classic difficult toprope that requires clipping a lone directional bolt. Bolt anchors below the top.

19. Rim Job 5.13a
The sport climb to the right.

20. Lactic Tactics and Blackout 5.10d and 5.12
You can't really toprope these prominent roof cracks.

21. Club Cafe 5.9
This climbs the bulging seam 10 feet right of *Lactic Tactics*. Long slings required.

22. Thwarting Gravity's Evil Efforts 5.11c

23. Pillar of the Community 5.10d
Climb the center of the cobbled pillar right of a deep chimney.

24. High Road to Antwerp 5.10a
Practice for the Diamond. The crack climb about five feet right of the chimney.

25. Wall of Gore 5.10d
The face between *Antwerp* and a black streak.

26. The Apparition 5.10d
This crack climb begins at a block 20 feet right of *Antwerp*.

27. Sedated Raccoon 5.10
Climb the left-hand side of the left water streak passing an arching crack up high.

28. Petting Zoo 5.10a
The black and green streak.

29. Fall Is in the Air 5.8
The beautiful finger crack in an open book. Look for a hole down low.

30. Fat Finger Frenzy 5.11b

Not to be missed, this long and steep crack climb might best be toproped with anti-swing directionals.

31. Young Wretches 5.10a

Start behind a block.

32. Face Full o' Bush 5.8

Climb the crack with a bush on a short west-facing wall.

33. Lick Crack 5.8

This is the finger and hand crack right of *Bush Crack*.

34. Polaroid 5.10a

This sport climb is easily identified as it climbs a long arete right of the previous routes. The anchor bolts are difficult to reach, so consider toproping from the tree.

35. Bonzoid Crack 5.8

This toprope ascends the slabs right of #34 and finishes left of left-facing corner.

36. Caucasoid Corner 5.9

Toprope this from rock tie-offs or gear.

37. Caucasoid Wall 5.12a

The face left of #38 avoiding the hole on the wall's left side.

38. Caucasoid Crack 5.10d

A bolted crack. Toprope from anchors beneath the summit.

39. Warren Piece 5.11 b/c

This is the beautiful bright green arete encountered as one heads towards the Projects Wall. Set up the anchors at the very top, not the large ledge at 3/4 height.

40. Antithesis 5.11d

The double cracks right of *Warren Piece*. Ditto on the ledge beta.

41. Skunk Buttress 5.10a

The short sport arete can be TR'd from bolt anchors.

Caucasoid Wall

THE C SECTION

This is one of Castlewood's more popular sport areas and is located past The Corner Blocks, an area not described in this guide, but identified by many difficult routes that begin from a corridor formed by blocks. This good-looking wall has a prominent black streak (*Black Brow* climbs this line) as well as a dead tree on the left side of the cliff.

Routes in the C-Section are given written descriptions from left to right starting near the dead tree. If you choose to use the tree as a descent path, be cautious of bees. Other access can be found on either side. The necessity to descend to the base of the routes makes this area unsuitable for children. All but the first two routes, *Tholean Web*, and *Wishbone Crack* are sport climbs and have bolt anchors. Long slings will work for #1 and #2.

1. Black Brow 5.11a
A toprope up the black water streak with a brow-shaped roof down low.

2. Warden Petes 5.10
A right-facing corner to a hole then up to the top.

3. Beta Slave 5.10c
The first of the bolted routes on an orange wall.

4. Patrick Hedgeclipper 5.11c
Five camouflaged bolts mark the way.

5. Entry Level 5.8
A wonderful route on juggy cobbles. Not to be missed.

6. Heavy Duty Judy 5.10c
Just right of a black streak. Classic.

7. Radiation Fear 5.11a
For reference only. The anchors are too low to toprope this three-bolt line.

8. First Dibs 5.10d
This route diagonals up and left so watch the swing thing.

9. Wishbone Crack 5.10a
The natural line that looks like a wishbone down low.

10. Tholean Web 5.12a
A difficult looking smooth wall can be toproped.

11. Korbomite Maneuver 5.12a
An excellent route with a boulder problem crux low and more difficulties up high. The upper left finish adds a letter grade.

12. Pebble Beach 5.11c/d
An interesting route that climbs near a slender water streak.

13. Quid Pro Cracks 5.11a
The righthand sport route with three bolts.

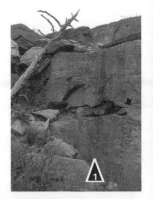

SEA WORLD

This beautiful streaked wall is north of the Vulture Walls and south of the C-Section. All routes have bolt anchors that can be reached from the top. The best downclimb is just past the Vulture Walls. (See overview map). As with many Castlewood cliffs, the base area is safe for kids, but the approach could be dangerous.

1. Tradewinds 5.11a/b

Six bolts define a line on the perimeter of the lefthand water streak.

2. Horse Latitudes 5.11b/c

The righthand side of the aforementioned streak.

3. Doldrums 5.12a

Left side; right streak.

4. It's a Nor'easter Outa Thar Sout'west 5.12a

5. Sea Breeze 5.11c

A 4-bolt line on the wall's right edge.

6. Sublerfuge 5.11d

A sport route right of the previous routes. Stellar. Not pictured.

7. Catch as Catch Can 5.11b

Even further right. Not pictured.

THE NORTH RIM

The easternmost part of Castlewood Canyon isn't as popular with climbers as its western counterpart. This may change with the development of a new sport crag near Wendell Spire. This area will also be of interest for toproping, as all but a few of the anchors can be reached from above. Climbs around the Wendell Spire tend to stack up in the harder grades.

Use the East entrance off of Highway 83 to reach the Inner Canyon. Descend the cliffs via the Inner Canyon Trail. Walk the trail along Cherry Creek to identify walls. Cherry Creek is more approachable and pleasant in this inner canyon, and the South Rim receives all-day shade, a nicety for hot summer days. Climbs in this area will be addressed as one moves away from the Picnic Parking Area, beginning with the North Rim routes. As the South Rim routes are located both east and west of the parking lot, they will be described in both directions. See the map for further details.

The Wendell Spire Crag has been left out of this book as its routes really aren't conducive to toproping, but may help you get your bearings. Wendell Spire is a one-pitch tower, which is detached from the main cliff by a few feet.

Dan hare helping the author research the grades.

CORPORATE VIEW BLOCK

The Corporate View Block is so named for its blocky appearance and its vantage point of the Corporate Walls which lie across the canyon to the southwest. Though the block itself houses several topropes, the anchors can be reached only by climbing other routes. At 5.5, *Joe's So Low* is the easiest way up or down. Three routes on the surrounding walls are the main attraction. Reaching the block requires some scrambling, as does reaching the anchors. A scramble left of *Scary Princess* provides a 4th class approach, as does the chimney behind *Sloping Screams*.

1. Fairy Princess 5.9

About eight feet north of the Block, climb a clean, pocketed south-facing wall.

2. Dry Hump 5.9

The left side of the west face. *Dry Hump* the detached block then enjoy the face.

3. Gridlocks 5.10d

The center route on the west face.

4. Joe's So Low 5.5

A pun on the way Joe climbed the crack. The best approach to the summit.

5. Amyosthenia 5.11a

A silly sport route.

6. Mom Deaf 5.11a

A worthy toprope.

7. Sloping Dreams 5.12a

Climb five feet left of the margin of the face.

THE PLAYGROUND

This enjoyable wall is located about a hundred meters east of the power lines. It is easily identified by the stone hoodoo reminiscent of Arches National Park. The best access to the anchors is via a scramble behind this balanced rock formation.

1. Black Slide 5.11a
A hand crack leads to a bolted water streak.

2. Playing Hookie 5.10b/c
Angle left past four bolts.

3. Problem Child 5.10
Not everyone who plays hookie is a problem child. A single bolt identifies this route right of *Hookie*.

4. Darys' Crack 5.8
Most easily toproped from gear.

5. Emerald Epitaph 5.10a
Climb near the thin S-shaped crack.

6. Pulling the Flake 5.10a
The crack formed from the partially detached flake.

7. High Flyer 5.9+
Hang on to shallow left-facing corners up the center of this south-facing wall.

8. Chinook 5.10b
A three-bolt climb starting on pockets.

9. Crack of the Past 5.10a
The beautiful corner.

10. Professor Plum with the Candlestick in the Conservatory 5.12a/b
Get a clue.

11. East Meets West 5.13a?
Climb the overhang and smooth wall right of *Professor Plum*.

12. Silmarillion 5.11b
The pumpy four-bolt line (sounds like an oxymoron) to the right of the cave-like area.

13. No Wimp Situation 5.11c
An overhanging crack with three bolts.

14. Parallax 5.11
Difficult beginning to a cake finale.

THE JUGGERNAUT AREA

The Juggernaut Area is easily identified by its location directly beneath the power lines. *Bat Face* is perhaps he finest 5.10 on this side of the Inner Canyon. The approach is long for Castlewood and once you leave the main trail, a bit of bushwhacking is involved. Anchor access is via a scramble on either side of the routes.

Good-looking slabs

1. Pipe Dreams 5.10

This sport route, not shown, is located on the lower tier, about a hundred feet west of the Juggernaut.

2. Pebbles and Bam Bam 5.9+

Another sport route that can be toproped. This one begins on the upper tier about 60 feet west of #3.

3. Rape, Pillage and Murder Wall 5.10a-d

The west face has several variations. One bolt. *Sweet Arete* (5.10d) is on the NW corner.

4. Seem to Seam 5.12a

After a jump start or a difficult problem, the route remains hard. Steeper than it seems.

5. Bat Face 5.10a

Holy handholds, Batman. An excellent bolted face climb.

6. Bat Wing 5.9

The wall right of *Bat Face* can be toproped.

7. Super Conductor 5.11a

8. Slab Happy 5.10

A short bolted 5.11a arete and a 5.10 face route can be toproped if you jump to the anchors.

SHAKESPEAREAN THEATER & REVOLUTION BUTTRESS

Not to be confused with the University of Colorado's Mary Rippon Theatre, home of the Colorado Shakespeare Festival. The approach is a bit longer than the jaunt from the University Hill to campus, but the climbing is worth the hike. The area is located just above and to the north of the juncture of the Inner Canyon Trail and Lake Gulch Trail. A large roof and black water streak help identify the climbs, which are generally harder sport routes. The Theater includes the routes left of the big roof, while locals refer to the right-hand routes as the Revolution Buttress. The hike isn't bad but might be a bit lengthy for small children.

The top is accessed on the east end of the buttress left of *Much Ado....* All routes on the Shakespearean Theater use bolt anchors, while routes 8, 9, and 11 require long slings for natural anchors.

1. Much Ado About Bolting 5.11d/5.12a
Follow a line of five bolts to a double-bolt anchor. Easily toproped from above.

2. King Fear 5.12
The thin crack with a bolt anchor over the top.

3. The Taming of the Shoe 5.12a
Another topropable sport climb with three bolts. To play fair, don't use the *King Fear* crack.

4. Rodeo and Juliet 5.11c/d
Essentially this toprope takes the fall line from *Taming's* anchors. Avoid the crack out right.

5. Shakespur 5.11a
This arete can be TR'd from bolts on top.

6. The Hangdogs of Verona 5.11d/5.12a
A worthy outing with the crux between a big cobble and a pocket. Bolts on top.

7. Wordy Drama 5.11d
Not named for this guidebook. Climb the obvious black water streak. Stemming is legal.

The Revolution Buttress

The Revolution Buttress is essentially the right side of the Shakespearean Theater. The routes tend to be significantly easier and require long slings for the anchors. Again, this might be a long and difficult walk for small children.

8. Butterfly McQueen's Birthday 5.9+

The face route immediately left of the upper roof wanders between two cracks.

9. Jamuary 5.9+

The third crack right of the big lower roof is flared and challenging.

10. The Revolution 5.10d

This route, just right of *Jamuary*, is identified by a high first bolt followed by three others. Bolt anchors on top.

11. The Resolution 5.9+

A little resolve goes a long way. This route ascends a scooped face and water streak about 10 feet right of *Revolution*.

12. Mind Meld 5.11a

This lonesome sport climb is found about 100 meters east of the Revolution Buttress on the next reasonably sized rock. Look for five welded cold shuts with a two-bolt anchor.

SOUTH RIM

The South Rim of the Inner Canyon is the shadiest area in Castlewood and for that reason is a good summer haunt. The Corporate Walls and The Realm of the Vesuvian Love Goddess offer some longer quality routes. The Honeycomb Spire area, though shorter and more limited for quality outings, can provide a quick after-work fix. See the overview map of Castlewood for locations. Other routes exist on this side of the canyon; however, they are not of the quality or concentration of the cliffs listed. Of note, however, are two easily toproped sport routes encountered when walking between the Corporate Walls and the Realm of the Vesuvian Love Goddess. *The Fully Clothed Edge* (encountered first) and *I Love You* are both easy 5.10 and worth climbing if in the area.

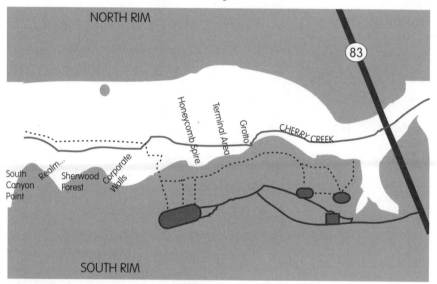

Ken Arledge on Hippopromis

HONEYCOMB SPIRE

Reach the Honeycomb Spire from the main parking area, (past the visitor center) take the easternmost trail that joins the rim trail. Follow this for about a hundred feet then head northeast to the top of the south rim. Walk along the rimrock to the east, keeping an eye out for a triangular block with a bolt on the top. This is the Honeycomb Spire. Most routes are on the surrounding cliffs and are toproped from a combination of bolts and trees. Approach time is about two minutes. Scramble to the base from the west or east. The base is not great for kids. Beware of poison ivy.

1. Mosaic 5.10
Ascends the face right of the offwidth. Single-bolt anchor can be backed up with cams.

2. Deathwidth 5.9-
The squeeze chimney/offwidth just north of the spire.

3. Collage 5.11
The face left of *Deathwidth*.

4. Holy Lamb 5.10
The NE arete of Honeycomb Spire. Back up the bolt on the slighly disconcerting summit.

5. Honey Crack 5.6
The crack on the east side of the spire.

6. Unreliable Skinhead 5.10a
The face left of *Honey Crack*.

7. Brain Drain 5.9
Begin on a block and climb an ugly corner crack.

8. Rosebud 5.12a
Begin on a block on the opposite arete of *Rhinocerock* and finish at the anchor bolt for that route.

9. Rhinocerock 5.10c
Start on the opposite side of the boulder; finish at the same bolt.

10. Hippopromis 5.10a
Climb the black streak to a single-bolt anchor (as always, back it up with the neighboring bolt).

11. Serpentine Crack 5.6
A wandering north-facing hand crack.

The Corporate Walls

The Corporate Walls provide a quiet setting for shaded topropes in the 5.10-5.12 range. Approach from the main parking area by walking west along the rim. These crags are the first major group of walls east of the power lines. They appear as different buttresses or three large corner systems. The best downclimb is directly beneath the power lines.

1. Explosion at the Ballbearing Factory 5.11a/b

This is the leftmost of two sport routes on the tallest wall. Bolts are just beneath the top.

2. O.S.H.A. Inspection 5.11a/b

Practically a twin of *Explosion*, this sport route climbs over an arching roof. O.S.H.A must insist on 3-bolt anchors.

3. Cogswell Cogs 5.10

Climb the first east-facing wall right of *O.S.H.A.* Begin on the left and angle right, avoiding the large hole in the center of the face. A little contrived but hey...

4. Affirmative Action 5.10

Race alone won't get you up this route. Climb the left side of the north-facing wall left of *Hostile Takeover.*

5. Hostile Takeover 5.12a

The third east-facing wall, the one closest to the powerlines, contains two good topropes with bolt anchors. This is the left line which ascends steep black rock.

6. Unincorporated Conglomerate 5.11

The right-hand toprope.

THE REALM OF THE VESUVIAN LOVE GODDESS

This is the first major group of east-facing cliffs west of South Canyon Point. The area is nestled in woods and isn't one of the more easily identified crags in Castlewood. Approaching from below is almost not an option, as the forest is rather dense and no trails exist. The Realm is clearly worth the visit, as it is stacked with routes in the 5.9-easy 5.11 range and sees shade on hot summer days. Approach from above via the rimrock and descend via a 4th class downclimb to the east of the flake from where routes 1-3 start.

descent   *dangerous loose block*

1. Babajoe Samarandanadadevi 5.11a

This is a toprope left of the bolted *Vesuvian Love Goddess*. Stay right of the horizontal scoops on the wall's left side. This route and the next two climbs begin in a corridor formed from a detached block and the cliff proper. The best descent involves a short scramble into this wide chimney.

2. Vesuvian Love Goddess 5.10d/11a

This woman has no problem getting dates. Bolt anchors on this toprope can also be used for its neighbors, if you don't mind swinging.

3. Alien Handshake 5.12

This is the toprope eight feet right of *Vesuvian Love Goddess*. To maintain the grade, avoid the right-hand edge of the face.

4. The Grip of an Android 5.9

This toprope begins just left of the sport route *Oof Roof.*

5. Oof Roof 5.10

A line of bolts marks a climb up the right side of an overhang.

6. Scills 5.7

A rather dirty corner crack about halfway up the wall marks this route. Can be toproped from the anchors on #7.

7. March of the Druids 5.9

A good 5.9 sport route that tackles (well, at least crosses) a tiny overhang.

8. My Fat Budgie 5.9+

Did the Vesuvian Love Goddess do this to you? This line climbs the right side of the east-facing wall right of a large chimney crack. The chimney crack and the face to the left of *Budgie* have been climbed, but a large loose block makes these unsafe.

9. Randolf's Party 5.10

This toprope ascends a nice north-facing wall right of the previous route.

10. Magic Mountain 5.8

The clean corner crack right of *Randolf's Party*.

11. Astral Static 5.11a

This is the next north-facing wall right of *Magic Mountain*.

12. The Impossible Crack 5.7

Not nearly as hard as the one in Boulder Canyon. This is the next corner/crack to the right of *Magic Mountain*.

13. Tick Talk 5.10a

Climb the center of the widest east-facing wall between *Impossible Crack* and the chimney.

14. INRI 5.11a

A contrived route that climbs the narrow north face avoiding the crack on the right and the edge on the left.

15. Fifteen Feet of Slack 5.8

Typical of distracted belayers. Climb the corner left of the chimney.

16. Canary Islands 5.11

This toprope is found on the large east-facing wall, best identified by *Monster Slot*, an arching chimney in the center of this wall. *Canary Islands* takes the left line on the wall left of the slot.

17. Straits of Madagascar 5.11c

Climbs the middle of the wall left of #18.

18. Monster Slot 5.9

A worthy struggle.

19. Fester Does Pugsley 5.10a

I can't even think about it. Climb the wall right of the slot.

20. Lords of Conquest 5.11a/b

Climb the left-hand side of a detached block.

MORRISON

The bouldering crag of Morrison is home to a pair of excellent topropes. You might not want to make a whole day of these two routes, but if you're in the neighborhood or wish to round out a day of bouldering, they're worth the effort.

Park on the road beneath the cliff and follow an obvious climber trail to the cliff. (See map).

Nautilus 5.10

This excellent and steep route climbs the main prow of the Nautilus.

Right of Nautilus 5.10

O.K. I admit I don't know the name of this route. Climb a steep wall to bolt anchors. The anchors aren't obvious from the ground.

Nautilus Toprope

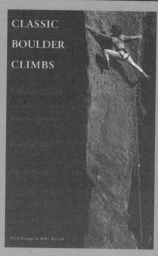

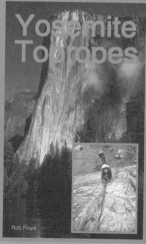

COLORADO SPRINGS

Heidi Knapp in the Garden of the Gods.
Photo Fred Knapp.

COLORADO SPRINGS

Colorado Springs, long a hotbed of Colorado climbing, offers many great toproping areas in and near the city. This guide covers four main areas:

The Garden of the Gods, a city park in Colorado Springs since 1910, lies to the west of the metropolis between Highway 24 and Garden of the Gods Road (both are Interstate exits). Exquisite sandstone fins and spires are showcased amid the dramatic backdrop of Pike's Peak. The sandstone of the Garden is diverse, with great friction and bomber holds next to gritty loose sections. Be careful climbing after rain (frequent in summer) as the rock becomes soft when wet.

For those inspired by solitude, North Cheyenne Canyon offers a more secluded setting while still being a roadside area. Mountain bikers and occasional passersby are the only distractions in this granite canyon.

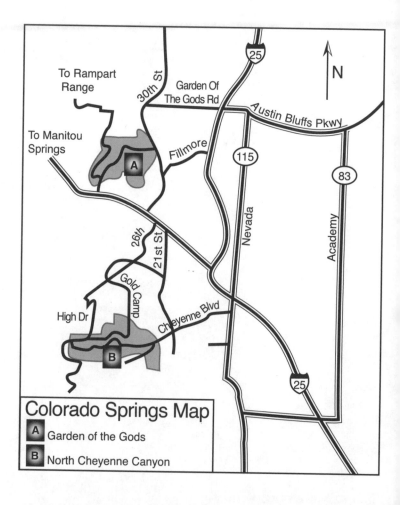

GARDEN OF THE GODS

The Garden of the Gods is the premier climbing area in Colorado Springs. This geologic marvel offers locals a convenient urban crag. The mostly paved short approaches and deluxe bathrooms make the Garden ideal for families. Children will enjoy exploring the trails, tunnels, and caves at ground level! Ancient bolt ladders, pitons, and pin scars testify to the area's long-term popularity with climbers. The park is very tolerant of climbers but asks that they refrain from using chalk and that they register with the park office (free and good for a calendar year). Lately, due to scrambling accidents, rangers actively patrol the park checking for permits. Please respect nesting raptors and signs for reclamation areas. Stay on trails. Be prepared to answer lots of questions from curious tourists and smile for their cameras.

See the map on the previous page for directions.

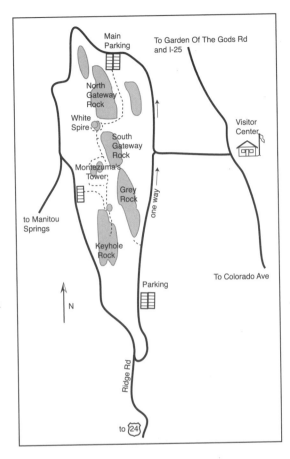

OVERVIEW OF THE GARDEN

WHITE SPIRE

White Spire is unique in this guide in that it can be toproped only by climbing a 5.6 route to the summit. It is, nonetheless, a popular toprope.

1. South Ridge 5.6

Bring gear to supplement the route's two pins if you decide to lead this.

2. West Face 5.8+

Follow the line of least resistance up the west face (pictured here).

3. Left Edge 5.10

Stay on the left side of the west face.

Martha Morris on White Spire

THE PRACTICE SLAB

The Practice Slab Routes 5.4-5.8

This is the long slab on the north end of the West Face of South Gateway Rock. Many popular topropes begin above the large ledge. Access the anchors via chopped steps on the right side of the slab.

White & Red Spires

Practice Slab

KEYHOLE ROCK

Keyhole Rock is the large nondescript formation on the southwest edge of the park. (See the overview photo and map). The rock contains an abundance of climbing on its multitiered east face. The first tier offers good toproping with relatively easy access to the anchors. The climbs can be approached from many parking areas, but it is best to approach from the main parking area. From the east, the first tier is hidden by another wall, as it rises from a gully. Enter the gully from the north near a small spire. The ledge from which to set up anchors can be approached by scrambles on either side. Back up the trees.

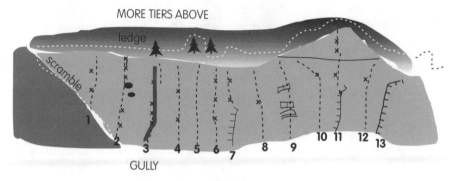

1. Left Face 5.11a

This short but steep route climbs past two drilled pitons.

2. Shock It To the Top 5.12b

A difficult endeavor protected by five pins. Creative use of trees and gear.

3. Waterchute Route 5.12a

The seemingly easy water groove proves more challenging than it appears. Tree anchors

4. Patty the Pig 5.10d

Some say this is the best route on the crag. Tree anchors.

5. Pig Dust 5.11d

No bolts on this route which is toproped from trees.

6. Angel Dust 5.10

Climbs past three pins. Tree anchors.

7. Rocket Dust 5.10

This route begins up a dihedral of sorts. Tree anchor.

8. Surprise 5.8

The neighboring route with a lonely bolt. You can still make use of the trees.

9. Sloping Shelves 5.7

This climbs the most featured part of the wall on rock that looks like bricks laid by a drunk mason. Gear.

10. New Improved Prodigal Son 5.8

Weird gear for anchors.

11. Morning After 5.10d

Start up the corner and tackle the headwall. Friends, etc. for the anchors

12. Face Route 5.6

One pin marks the spot. Gear anchors.

13. Dihedral Route 5.9

One fixed pin on this climb. Ditto.

KEYHOLE ROCK

scramble

1
2
3
4
5
6 7 8

GRAY ROCK

The southern terminus of Gray Rock is home to some of the Garden's best topropes. Like the sport climbs on the east face, these routes take advantage of the best rock in the Garden.

Approach from the parking area south of Gray Rock. Walk down the road until an obvious trail parallels a creek bed and leads to the cliff. Three sets of bolt anchors can be accessed by a sketchy scramble up a slab to the left of the routes. Begin just left of a gully and climb to a slabular ledge, which can be traversed to the bolt anchors. The third and westernmost set of bolt anchors involves scrambling up and over a small ridge. It is best to rappel from the anchors, rather than downclimb the slab.

Gray Rock Topropes

South Face of Gray Rock

North Cheyenne Canyon

North Cheyenne Canyon, though often neglected in modern times, has a long climbing history. The area was used by the military as a training ground and demonstration area. Pin scars and paint dots from old Harvey T. Carter routes are evident on the Pinnacle Practice Wall, as are fixed Army ring angles and an occasional old bolt.

The rock is a pink granite reminiscent of Joshua Tree. When it erodes it forms a coarse talus that makes for hazardous hiking. As gonzo mountain bikers race down the trails, you'll wonder at the road rash risk (say that fast) they are chancing.

North Cheyenne Canyon, though not extensive, is ultimately worth a visit by Front Range topropers. Pine forests, a babbling brook, short approaches, quality granite, and a general absence of crowds, make this a hidden gem.

Sonia Knapp on the Pinnacle Practice Wall

The Army Demonstration Area

The Army Demonstration Area consists of several crags in the periphery of an abandoned amphitheater. The primary toproping crags are the Roadside Crag and the Amphitheater Wall. To reach these areas, drive 0.7 miles from the crosswalk at the canyon entrance to a good pull-out on the right.

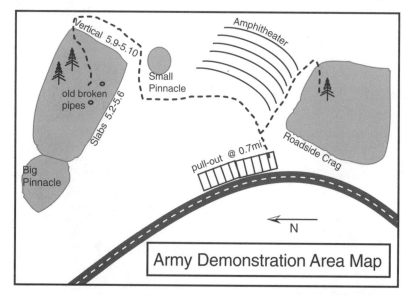

Army Demonstration Area Map

THE ROADSIDE CRAG 5.7-5.9

Just above the road is a clean granite slab that offers topropes in the 5.7-5.9 range. Getting to the top is mildly tricky. Ascend to the top of the amphitheater via the obvious steps, then scramble through a groove until it is possible to walk down to the tree anchors. Use caution as the top of this cliff is quite grainy. The Roadside routes aren't named, but variations are obvious. See the map below for parking information. The white square on the photo at right indicates the climbing area.

THE AMPHITHEATER WALL

To the north of the amphitheater and right of a small pinnacle is a clean east-facing slab offering relatively easy routes that can be toproped from trees. (At one time, large pipes were placed in the rock and served as anchors, but they have been vandalized).

The more vertical wall that is passed en route to the anchors offer routes in the 5.9-5.10 range. Bring 30-50 foot slings for all routes.

PINNACLE PRACTICE WALL

The Pinnacle Practice Wall parking area lies 0.1 miles up from the Army Demonstration Area. Park across from a stone bridge and follow the obvious trail. The Pinnacle Practice Wall has seen recent development with the addition of some new bolted sport routes. These routes, like their traditional neighbors, make excellent toprope problems. Unfortunately, a fourth class scramble is required to get to the top of the cliff. Lower from anchors or rappel to get off.

1. The Roof Route 5.9+
2. Aid Crack 5.10a
3. New Face Route 5.11b
4. The Bolt Route 5.11d/5.12a

Climbs past four bolts to a bolt anchor. The hangers are missing on the anchors, but the trees suffice.

5. Over the Arch 5.10a/b

Climb a left-angling crack system over the arch. Tree anchors.

6. Dihedral Route 5.8
7. Bolted 9 5.9
8. The Arete Route 5.11

SOUTH PLATTE AREA

Heidi Knapp on Left Handed Jew at Turkey Perch

SOUTH PLATTE

Turkey Rocks is arguably the best crag in the South Platte region. Splitter cracks on featured granite are the main attractions. Simply put — every climber should visit this area!

Elevenmile Canyon lies about 40 miles from the Springs and provides an excellent opportunity to climb and camp in a less populated setting. Summer swimming holes make for a great escape from the heat. The River Wall, in fact, is perched just above excellent swimming holes. Take some time to get off the beaten path and discover your own topropes on the many undocumented cliffs and boulders.

TURKEY ROCKS/TURKEY PERCH

With an excellent range of difficulties, exposure, and route lengths (as well as a close proximity to South Denver and Colorado Springs) Turkey Rocks can be a busy destination. This is a great place to take in an alpine setting on a hillside strewn with lichened boulders. The hike is steep but short and the dirt road approach — navigable by most 2WD vehicles on a dry day — provides justification for your SUV.

Though many of the routes are multi-pitch, the Turkey Perch features a slew of topropable classics. The majority of the routes are splitter crack climbs, though some excellent face routes exist. Most climbs can be toproped from tied-off boulders and trees, but a few pieces may help directionally. Bring 20-30 foot slings. The base is comfortable and generally safe for kids, though the nearby boulderfields may encourage exploration. With so many classic routes in the 5.7 to 5.9 range, this is the spot to hone your crack skills.

Approach Turkey Rocks from Denver by heading to the town of Westcreek via Deckers on Colorado Highway 67 (see map). Turn off 67 on the gravel road that leads to Westcreek proper and head another 0.8 miles south. Turn onto Stump Road (Road 68) and follow this for 2.5 miles to Forest Road 360. Reset your odometer and continue along this road (passing Big Turkey Campground at 1.7 miles) to an unsigned road on the left at 2.5 miles. Follow this road for about three quarters of a mile to the Turkey Rocks parking area. An obvious trail leads to the crags after about ten to fifteen minutes of hiking.

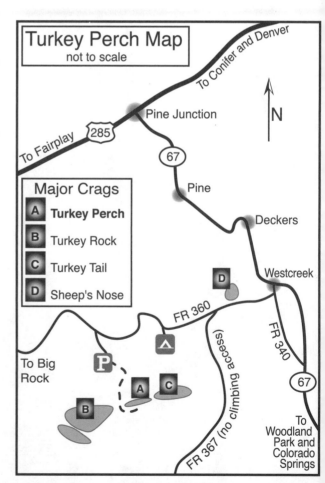

Turkey Perch Map
not to scale

To Conifer and Denver

Pine Junction

285 To Fairplay

67

N

Pine

Deckers

Major Crags

A **Turkey Perch**

B Turkey Rock

C Turkey Tail

D Sheep's Nose

Westcreek

FR 360

FR 340

67

To Big Rock

P

To Woodland Park and Colorado Springs

FR 367 (no climbing access)

Turkey Perch is reached by veering left and a slight bit down once you've reached the saddle. To access the top of the cliff, scramble up either side.

For more information, check out Ken Trout's excellent topo guide *SOUTH PLATTE ROCK.*

TURKEY PERCH

1. Bloody Englishman 5.8
The Brit didn't tape his hands. A quality hand and finger crack on the left side of the crag.

2. Liquid Acrobat 5.12a
This popular and difficult toprope begins up a fingertip lieback and steps right across a thin blank wall to another tips seam.

3. Unnamed One 5.6
Right of *Liquid Acrobat* is another crack climb.

4. Unnamed Two 5.6
Not as good as the other routes on the Perch.

5. Reefer Madness 5.8
You'll smoke this one if your jamming skills are up to par. Finish left up the face.

6. Ragger Bagger 5.8
Good crack in a left-facing corner.

7. Gobble Up 5.9
An excellent route for improving fist crack and offwidth technique. Set the toprope so the rope doesn't get gobbled up in the crack. You'll need a 60 meter rope and long slings to toprope this long route.

8. Stiff Little Fingers 5.11c
The thin bolt-protected face can be toproped. Also requires a 60 meter rope and long slings.

9. Steppenwolf 5.9
Considered by many to be the finest route on the crag, this brilliant handcrack terminates with a face climbing finish. Like its neighbors, this classic requires long slings and a 60 meter cord.

10. Unnamed Three 5.8
The rightmost crack in the shallow chimney right of *Steppenwolf.*

11. Honkey Jam 5.7
Quality route on excellent hand jams.

*Jane Klein finessing
Big Ledge Face Toprope Two*

12. Left Handed Jew 5.7

Follow the beautiful hand crack to a small roof, then step left and finish up the crack above.

*The following three routes can be toproped from the top of the big block right of *Left Handed Jew*. The top of the block, however, isn't conducive to anchor placements. You must place anchors in cracks behind and to the side of the block. The safest and easiest way to get to the top of the block is to swing over to it from *Left Handed Jew*.

13. Big Ledge Toprope Crack 5.8

From the big ledge right of the previous route, toprope the left-facing corner. Not pictured.

14. Big Ledge Face Toprope One 5.11

Toprope a route from the big ledge near the left side of the short face. Not pictured.

15. Big Ledge Face Toprope Two 5.11a

Toprope a route from the big ledge near the right side of the short face. The more you use the right side of the arete, the easier the climbing. Not pictured.

ELEVENMILE CANYON —
THE RIVER WALL

Located about 40 miles from Colorado Springs, Elevenmile Canyon is a stunning granite climbing area with a variety of features from large domes to short sport crags. The River Wall, with its short approach, accessible anchors and quality rock is the main toproping venue in Elevenmile Canyon. During the summer, the river offers a refreshing place to take a dip. The base of the wall, however, isn't suitable for small children.

To reach Elevenmile Canyon, take I-25 to the US 24 exit in Colorado Springs. Follow Highway 24 through Woodland Park (a little confusing — stay left) to the town of Lake George. Take a left at Park County Road 96 and follow this for about a mile to the Elevenmile Canyon Park entrance station. Pay the $4.00 fee and continue 6.2 miles to the River Wall (just past a bridge). The River Wall is best approached by crossing the bridge and following a climbers trail up the mound then back down to the river and over to the cliff. At high water an alternative approach may prove better.

The quickest access to the top of the River Wall is found at the wall's left side. Look for an obvious chimney with a large chockstone forming a tunnel. If you do not wish to scramble, you can access the top by walking east until it becomes possible to hike to the top. Long slings are needed.

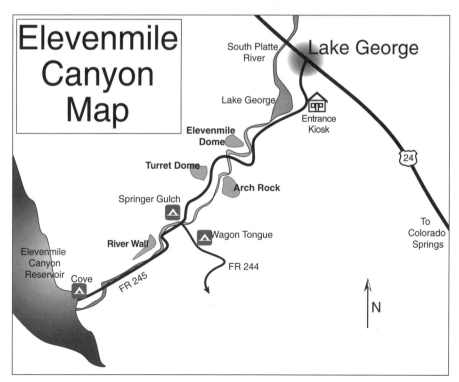

1. Easy Slab Routes 5.5-5.7
The left side of the River Wall offers vast opportunities to toprope on featured, albeit licheny, slabs.
Natural anchors with long slings. Beware some grainy loose rock up top.

2. Wingless Angel 5.11
A toprope problem about three meters left of *Captain Cod Piece*.

3. Captain Cod Piece 5.11c
This is the steep finger crack that starts behind the trees. Shady and pumpy.

4. Simple Minds 5.12b
This mixed route can be toproped from the top of the cliff, but the angle makes this somewhat
inconvenient.

5. Darylect 5.12c
This is the bolted route right of the trees. It can also be toproped from natural anchors.

6. Loaf and Jug 5.7
This route essentially follows the path of least resistance on the large slab that forms the left wall of a
huge open book. Boundless variations exist on the pretty piece of rock. Tree anchors.

7. Life on the Run 5.10a
Begin at the right margin of the huge roof and follow the right-trending finger crack/groove.
A directional makes for less swing potential.

8. Running Man 5.9+
This line takes the weakness right of *Life on the Run*. It is possible to toprope both from the
same anchor.

9. Blood Brothers 5.12a
This boulder problem on a rope follows the slab and groove to a crux bolted bulge. Back up the single
bolt anchor off natural anchors or nearby cam placements.

10. Flat Earth Society 5.11a-c
This route begins on the steep slab and follows bolts past a crack to the bulge above. The difficulty can
be reduced by veering right of the bolt line. Getting to the anchor bolts can be a wee bit dicey.

11. Pumping Chuck 5.11c
This featured west-facing bolted wall is a worthy outing. Sustained. The easy-to-reach two-bolt anchor
requires short slings.

12. Skid Marks 5.11c
The rib right of *Pumping Chuck* provides an exercise in balance. Shares anchors with the previous route.

THE BEST OF FRONT RANGE TOPROPES

(OR RECOMMENDATIONS FROM THE AUTHOR)

BEST OVERALL AREAS:
1. Grocery Store Wall (Castlewood Canyon)
2. Happy Hour Crag (Boulder Canyon)
3. Turkey Perch (South Platte Area)
4. Table Mountain (Golden)

BEST QUICK AFTER WORK SPOTS:
1. Pumpkin Rock (Flagstaff Mountain)
2. The Bolt Wall (Horsetooth Reservoir)
3. Morrison (Denver Area)
4. Practice Rock (Boulder Canyon)
5. White Spire (Garden of the Gods)
6. The Brick Wall (Boulder Canyon)

BEST PLACE FOR BEGINNERS
1. Gregory Canyon Amphitheater (Flatirons)
2. Mary's Lake (Estes Park Area)
3. Gray Rock Toprope Wall (Garden of the Gods}
4. Crown Rock (Flagstaff Mountain)

BEST WEEKEND GETAWAY
1. Turkey Perch (South Platte Area)
2. Elevenmile Canyon (South Platte Area)
3. Ironclads/Punk Rock (Estes Park Area)

BEST VARIETY OF GRADES AT A SINGLE CRAG
1. Table Mountain (Golden)
2. Grocery Store Wall (Castlewood Canyon)
3. Ironclads/Punk Rock (Estes Park Area)
4. Duncan's Ridge (Horsetooth Reservoir)

BEST CRACK CLIMBING
1. Turkey Perch (South Platte Area)
2. King Conqueror (Flagstaff Mountain)
3. Mental Block (Boulder Canyon)
4. Practice Rock (Boulder Canyon)

Sleepers (quality crags you hear little about)

1. Little Crag (Boulder Canyon)
2. Ironclads/Punk Rock (Estes Park Area)
3. Pinnacle Practice Wall (North Cheyenne Canyon)
4. Keyhole Rock (Garden of the Gods)
5. C Section (Castlewood Canyon)
6. Woods Quarry (Flatirons)

Best place with Bolt Anchors

1. Ironclads/Punk Rock (Estes Park Area)
2. The Brick Wall (Boulder Canyon)
3. Grocery Store Wall (Castlewood Canyon)
4. The Cube (Flatirons)
5. C Section (Castlewood Canyon)

Best Lapping Routes (difficult)

1. Pumpkin Rock (Flagstaff Mountain)
2. East Overhang (Eldorado Canyon)
3. Little Twin Owl Finger Crack (Estes Park Area)
4. Couch Potato (Flatirons, Boulder)

Routes You Absolutely Shouldn't Miss

1. West Bench Topropes 5.3-5.7 (Gregory Canyon Amphitheater)
2. Idle Hands 5.6 (The Boulderado, Boulder Canyon)
3. Left Handed Jew 5.7 (Turkey Perch)
4. Honkey Jam 5.7 (Turkey Perch)
5. Grins 5.8 (Happy Hour Crag, Boulder Canyon)
6. Twofers 5.8 (Happy Hour Crag, Boulder Canyon)
7. Bloody Englishman 5.8 (Turkey Perch)
8. Entry Level 5.8 (C Section, Castlewood Canyon)
9. March of Dimes 5.9 (Eldorado Canyon)
10. Classic Finger Crack 5.9 (Elephant Buttresses, Boulder Canyon)
11. Tough Situation 5.9 (Elephant Buttresses, Boulder Canyon)
12. Finger Crack 5.9 (Nip and Tuck, Boulder Canyon)
13. Deck Chairs on the Titanic 5.9 (North Table Mountain)
14. Little Flatiron 5.9-5.10 (Flagstaff Mountain)
15. Dementia 5.10 (Happy Hour Crag, Boulder Canyon)
16. South Face 5.10 (Brick Wall, Boulder Canyon)
17. Nautilus 5.10 (Morrison)
18. Heavy Duty Judy 5.10 (C Section, Castlewood Canyon)
19. Aid Crack 5.10 (Cob Rock, Boulder Canyon)
20. Regular Route 5.11 (Practice Rock, Boulder Canyon)
21. Pumpkin Rock 5.11 (Flagstaff Mountain)
22. Finger Crack 5.11 (Little Twin Owls)
23. Yellow Christ 5.12 (The Cube, Flatirons)

INDEX